Shaker Ghost Stories from Pleasant Hill, Kentucky

by

Thomas Freese

authorHOUSE™

1663 LIBERTY DRIVE, SUITE 200
BLOOMINGTON, INDIANA 47403
(800) 839-8640
WWW.AUTHORHOUSE.COM

Laurie Cochran.

First published by AuthorHouse 08/02/05

ISBN: 1-4208-5072-5 (sc)

Library of Congress Control Number: 2005905251

Printed in the United States of America
Bloomington, Indiana

This book is printed on acid-free paper.

Contents

Centre Family Dwelling

Introduction

The best stories are true and personal stories. I came to know Pleasant Hill in 1990 as a visitor and tourist. At that time I was living in Santa Fe, New Mexico, and traveling in the Eastern half of the United States. I was looking for a new home after having lived in Santa Fe for 11 years. Shakertown was one of the drawing forces that led me to move to the nearby Bluegrass area, Lexington, Kentucky. At that time I was aware of Shakertown being an oasis of rural land and nineteenth century history, quaint and quiet.

But it wasn't until a friend invited me to a nature walk and talk at Shakertown, and afterwards I heard and joined the Pleasant Hill Singers, that I came to know the magnetic pull of peacefulness and spirituality that is the core of the Shaker experience. Some of the singers are also employees and those seasoned workers used that exact term, "Shaker experience", to describe the initiatory and direct encounter with the Shaker spirits. I was truly mesmerized by the accounts of active spirit presence at Pleasant Hill, and it seemed a sacred duty to hear those stories and take it as a personal mission to record them.

I feel that the hallmark of a true ghost story is its simplicity; they may be odd, perhaps, but oftentimes the encounter is no more than hearing a voice, smelling a fragrance, or seeing a glimpse of a Shaker figure. And there is hardly a visit to Shakertown that is without an updated account of a friend or guest or fellow Shaker singer having had another Shaker experience. Nearly all of the stories that I've heard involve Shaker spirits true to their collective character that they displayed in life—helpful, inspired, and dedicating their lives to God and service to others.

Interpreters crossing village lane

I am accepting of the reality of ghosts and spirits; I already was a believer when at age 40 I joined the Shaker singers. I have countless times since childhood experienced the presence of ghosts and I once saw one. My mental inclination is to believe in ghosts, faeries, psychic phenomenon and much more. Thus, in a sense, I don't really need the direct spirit encounter; I am pleased to hear others tell their tales which verifies my notion of reality. I have a collection of ghost stories from the world outside of Pleasant Hill too; I believe that the entire world and any and every household can be visited by spirits. Ghosts carry their mortal personality onward through the death experience; their post-transition character and actions are compatible with their pre-death inclinations and predisposition. Thus some ghosts may play out their drama of fear or territorial defensiveness. Other spirits may linger and be a source of love and support.

I believe that the communication and behavior of ghosts is purposeful; they show an intention to gift a visit to a certain person for a certain reason at a certain time in a certain manner. I've found this true in ghostly encounters anywhere, including Shakertown. We all feel their presence, some of us see and hear them, and they have a reason for creating the encounter...if nothing else than to say, "I am here, I am real, I have something to say or share." Those of you who have heard stories of families with haunted houses also know that the interactions of the relationships between the living and the living-in-spirit can be every bit as layered, humorous, and testy as those we experience with our friends and family. Ghosts utilize symbolic communication, metaphor, and humor.

The *Course in Miracles* states that we teach what we have learned. I believe that the spirits are encouraging us to keep an open mind and open heart. They have made the life transition into pure spirit. The expansive universe begins in our own mind, and the reminders to our own spirit essence may be little, subtle things along the way. If you have had spirit encounters, then you know and understand. If you haven't yet seen, heard or felt a ghost, then just keep an open mind and heart to believe others when they say that they heard a singing in the Meeting House when "nobody" was there.

North Lot ruins

CHAPTER 1

The Shakers at Pleasant Hill

I had no idea of the extensive history of the spiritual community known as the Shakers, and many people have very limited knowledge, if any, of the Shakers. Some of that limited information may be skewed to view only their celibacy as their downfall. However, the Shakers prospered, thrived and their commitment to non-sexual relations was but one facet of a deep love for life, God and their fellow mortals. When visiting Shakertown, and despite the material evidence of industry and labor, it nevertheless takes a certain amount of imagination and investigation to see just how successful the Shakers were in living right livelihood, creating harmony of spirit and body, and implementing social and gender justice.

The members of the United Society of Believers in Christ's Second Appearing were from Manchester,

England. Led by an uneducated but charismatic woman named Ann Lee, she sailed with a small group of believers to New York in 1774. After initial struggles, their group grew with evangelizing efforts and soon sent missionaries to spread the Shaker faith and to establish communities set apart from the world. The Shakers created 19 utopian villages based on equality of the sexes, pacifism and religious freedom. They particularly thrived during the first half of the nineteenth century. They believed in common ownership of property, celibacy, public confession of sins, and separation from the world.

The industrious Shakers thrived; their motto was, "Hands to work, and hearts to God." Pleasant Hill, Kentucky was founded in 1805 and within three decades became the third largest of the Shaker communities, with 500 members. The Civil War, shifting markets, declining membership and inadequate leadership lead to a decline in the latter 1800's. The last Pleasant Hill Shaker passed away in 1923.

Pleasant Hill's restoration was begun in 1966. A visitor will find 33 restored buildings and some 3,000 acres of original Shaker land. A thriving historic site, Shakertown is located 25 miles southwest of Lexington, near the dramatic limestone palisades of the Kentucky River. The village has overnight accommodations, a craft store, farm and gardens, and a number of educational programs. The educational programs include herb classes, music programs, nature walks, Civil War encampments, draft farm animal husbandry, archaeological talks and specialized Shaker studies. Shaker craft classes teach participants how to make nesting boxes, chairs, brooms and rugs. Shaker interpreters wear Shaker-like garb and make brooms, weave, cook, drive wagons, make shoes and provide Shaker song and dance in the historic Meeting House. The men are dressed in dark trousers with a vest (black or navy blue in color). Under their simple vest they wear a long-sleeved white shirt. When they are outdoors, the men have a sturdy, straw hat with a flat, oval top. The women interpreters reproduce the Shaker clothing with a blue dress and a white apron. They have a white modesty scarf that crosses the bosom and show respect with sun cap or bonnet. Some of the singers wear a completely white dress to imitate the Shaker women's Sunday meeting attire. Both men and women wear simple black shoes without buckles.

A number of the sightings of Shaker spirits were assumed to be encounters with Pleasant Hill employees who were dressed in Shaker style clothing. The irony is that of the employees recreating Shaker devotion to work while their Spiritual brethren, the Shaker ghosts, are active in their midst.

For ten years I have been traveling to Mercer County, near Harrodsburg, Kentucky, to Shakertown. Even when I worked as an artist in residence and was a four-hour drive away, I was still motivated to join with the Shaker singers and be once again inspired by the Shaker music. We would talk about the Shakers; there was always some new bit of history or biography to learn about Mother Ann or the Pleasant Hill Shakers. The stories of the lives of those pioneers in land and adventurers in spirit were amazing to us. And with each singers rehearsal or winter retreat, there were more tales to tell of the Shaker spirits. They were just as active as us!

Stone fence and orchard

1820 Meeting House   Photo by Don Pelly

CHAPTER 2

"Are there any ghosts around here?"

The Shakers wrote over 30,000 songs and some of those tunes were written at Pleasant Hill. When I joined the Shaker singers, I found that each gathering was a chance to learn a new song, and some of those songs were very inspiring to us singers. The titles reveal the Shakers' devotion to love, honest living, and openness to the spirit of God moving through them: "Now's the Time to Enter In", "Since We are Called to Liberty", "Who Will Bow and Bend Like a Willow", "Pretty Love and Union", "I'll Beat my Drum", and "I'm on My Way to Zion". We performed in costume throughout the year, and once a year in the winter we had our singers' retreat. We wore jeans and enjoyed the relaxing atmosphere and time to become better friends. We had new singing material to learn, but on breaks and on Saturday night we could gather around and talk about how the Shakers influenced us. On February 11, 1997, we were in the basement of the West Lot Dwelling, gathered in couches and chairs around the cozy fire. One of the seasoned singer/employees mentioned their Shaker experience of being accompanied by a spirit presence in village, and the stories from our group flowed along for several hours. When I expressed my interest to know more, I was given names of other Pleasant Hill workers; I was determined that the stories of Shaker ghosts not be lost.

It took another year, though, of hearing more stories and getting some encouragement from friends, to get up the courage to commit to the task of interviewing folks I didn't know. I asked and was given permission by officials at Pleasant Hill to speak with their employees about their experiences. So in the spring of 1998 I carried a tape recorder and notebook and began to follow leads in interviewing people in person or by phone to obtain their Shaker ghost stories. My search led me around the village at Pleasant Hill, to a bakery in nearby Harrodsburg, and out to various other states to contact visitors from Tennessee, California, and Ohio. I was never quite sure where the ghost stories from Shakertown would pop up. I happened to be in Nicholasville, Kentucky, at the Nicholasville Boot Store. As the shop owner was steaming the brim on my hat, I mentioned that I was writing a book on Shaker ghost stories. The man did not seem surprised, and actually reported an incident involving a man he knew.

His friend had been working at Shakertown for a Lexington construction and remodeling company. The shop owner's friend was working on a window and his arms were stretched up to use both hands on a tool. Neither hand was available to hold on to the window frame, as he had one leg dangling outside and the other leg inside the structure. Suddenly, he felt himself lose his balance and start to fall out of the window but an invisible hand grabbed his ankle and saved him from a disastrous fall.

One day, when I was taking a walk around the village with a friend, we stopped by the Cooper's Shop. Employee Connie Carlton is interesting to visit and watch make wooden buckets and tools. Connie went through the barrier gate, closing it behind him. While he walked over to the other side of the room where he did his craft demonstrations, my friend and I watched the barrier gate again open and close. When something like that happens, our mind is only too willing to put it into our experiential/mental File 13. In other words, the rational mind simply says, "That didn't happen."

I asked Connie if he had any ghostly encounters while working at Shakertown. Connie told of one event that happened to him in the nearby East Family Dwelling in 1994.

"I went over there one evening to use the downstairs restroom. As one comes into the first, big room, there are two doors that were left open. This happened before the Shaker Life Exhibit was set up. I was the only one in the building. As I came back out I was walking close to the door on the left side. The door slammed shut, right behind my heels. You couldn't have grabbed it and shut it any faster. It was like something said, 'You get out of here--you're on <u>my</u> turf!' It made the hair stand up on my neck. No other doors or windows were open. And there wasn't any reason for it--no gust of wind. I never would have thought about it if the door had swung around real slowly; but, it was like someone was trying to kick me out of the house. There are a lot of things you can't explain."

Dixie Huffman, Betty Jo Peavler
& Connie Carlton

Connie was working on his cedar and sassafras wooden buckets in April 1999 when a few overnight guests asked him to help start up their car with his jumper cables. The guests were a woman from Tennessee and her adult daughter. After assisting them, the woman perhaps felt relaxed enough to ask Connie the question, "Are there any strange happenings around here?"

Connie asked the woman just what she meant by 'strange things' and the woman confided, "Well, like ghosts in the village." She then told about her stay the previous night in a room in the West Family Sister's Shop.

"My daughter was asleep in her bed and I was getting ready for bed. I know that I had bolted shut our door to the hallway. I was wearing my nightgown and I was in the bathroom. The bathroom door was open just a little."

"While I was in the bathroom I heard our door open. I listened as footsteps sounded across the room. Then I heard the things I had set on the bedside table being lifted up and set down, one by one."

The guest told Connie that she and her daughter ended up sleeping in the same bed that night.

It seems that every Shaker building has had unusual occurrences. It was in the East Family Sister's Shop that some employees heard sounds in supposedly vacant rooms. Close to the Cooper's Shop lies the East Family Sister's Shop, built in 1855. There are weaving and spinning demonstrations on the first floor; and, as in a number of the restored buildings, there are guest lodgings above. One of the interpreters tells of sounds of the loom being worked at night. Those rooms are locked at six o'clock, but people who stay in the guest rooms upstairs have often heard the sounds of the shuttle and beating board. Although there are never any employees working on the looms at night, people have heard someone slamming on the looms.

A man who has worked in maintenance for ten years at Shakertown is nicknamed 'Tucker'. Tucker has worked below the floorboards of the East Family Sister's Shop and he has heard "bumps and stomping."

East Family Sister's Shop

Edith Allen Ransdell worked for 13 years in the East Family Sister's Shop. She demonstrated both spinning and weaving in two separate rooms across the hall from each other. As she went from one room to another she would often feel a presence, perhaps a female spirit, which would follow her from one room to another--but always stopping at the door of each room.

Rose Sorrell, the co-owner of the Harrodsburg Bakery, started working at Shakertown when she was fifteen years old. She worked in the gift shop, which was first housed in the Farm Deacon's Shop. After she'd worked there for two years, the gift shop was moved to its present location in the Carpenter's Shop. On a lovely summer's day in 1998, I drove the twenty minute drive from Shakertown to meet Rose and hear her Shaker ghost stories. Rose is a friendly soul and encouraged me to keep collecting the ghost stories; she helped by giving me some more names of those she knew had Shaker experiences.

Rose Sorrell told of a time when a third shift maintenance worker was at the East Family Brethren's Shop. The East Family Brethren's Shop is located in the east part of the village. The Shaker community of Pleasant Hill was divided into five communal families; and each family had its own dwellings and shops. For example, there is the Centre Family, the East Family and the West Family Dwellings, etc.

The worker was trying to help two guests get into the building. The exterior door simply has a latch to lift up and is not locked. He could not budge the latch, and he even tried to leverage it open with a crowbar. Some guests, upstairs, heard the sounds and came downstairs. They opened the door from the inside with no problem.

One former employee of Shakertown tells about Lee Releford, a man who formerly worked for the housekeeping department at Pleasant Hill. He went every day to the Tanyard Brick Shop (just down the hill from the East Family Brethren's Shop) to pick up the linen. When putting his key in the door, the door did not open. He felt that he needed to ask permission: "Okay, can I come in?" Then he'd turn the key, and the door would open. He said that this happened every time he went down there, and it <u>only</u> happened to him. When another Pleasant Hill employee took his key down there one day--they were able to open the door without any difficulty.

Tanyard Brick Shop

One day, one of the Pleasant Hill maintenance workers and a few other men drove down to the Tanyard Brick Shop to do work on the second floor. They entered a vacant building, as there were no guests staying in the rooms at that time; no other vehicles were parked outside. From their vantage point in the second floor room, and with all the windows on that floor, they would have seen or heard a visitor coming into the Tanyard. They saw no visitors or other workers, but when they came back downstairs they were surprised to find a log in the middle of the floor.

The largest building in the East Village is the East Family Dwelling. Built in 1817, this brick building has many rooms for overnight guests. During our Shaker singer retreats, I have stayed in various rooms throughout the East Family Dwelling, from the floor just above ground level, overlooking the village lane, to the fourth floor rooms tucked up near the attic rooms. A former employee tells of a door that simply didn't want to stay locked! It was the bathroom door to a room on the top floor--the fourth floor of the East Family Dwelling. She also recalls a restless rocking chair on the third floor of the East Family Dwelling: "It would often be seen rocking back and forth."

Another village 'hot spot' is the Trustee's Office. The Trustee's Office was built in 1839, and was the center of much activity, having served as the place for contact with the outside world. Here the society's trustees, those leaders who served as liaisons to the 'world,' lived and entertained visitors. Food and clothing were dispensed to the poor, and souls interested in becoming Shakers were counseled. The Trustee's Office is currently the site of much activity, containing a number of guest rooms and several very busy dining rooms. Graceful wooden staircases spiral up near the entrance to the dining area. We Shaker singers have often been given complimentary meals there during our retreats.

Bruce Herring is the captain of the Dixie Belle riverboat, which is owned and operated by Shakertown. Bruce pilots the Dixie Belle on the Kentucky River, taking visitors on a short cruise from the Shaker landing. He is an entertaining and knowledgeable guide for his passengers. Bruce had previously worked at the front desk at Pleasant Hill, which used to be located in the Trustee's Office. He remembers a time about 7 years ago when he was totally alone in that building. It was winter and there were no guests or employees in the village.

"I was working a shift from eight in the evening until eight in the morning. At that time the village was actually closed to visitors. But on two separate occasions I heard people walking around. I also heard a female voice singing. These sounds came from right above me, on the second floor. I walked out into the hallway...and I found no one there."

Trustee's Office

When I visited Shakertown in the summer of 1998, I wandered into the dining area of the Trustee's Office and asked the waiters and waitresses if they had any ghost stories to share. One employee remembered a young African-American lady who worked in the dining room. The woman saw a woman in white 'floating' down the back stairs. The waitress dropped her serving tray and screamed, "There's someone out there! There's someone out there!" It was reported that the young woman clocked out and promptly left for the day.

Sarah Moran has worked as a waitress in the dining room of the Trustee's Office for many years. "Recently, and many times previously, I've heard my name called. When I look around, nobody is there.

That only happens on the porch. One time after we had closed I went into the east room of the Trustee's Office. There was nobody else in there. I had set up the tables with all their tableware and glasses and napkins. But later, when I went back into the east room I noticed the silverware on the two larger tables had been messed up. A lot of times things are just out of place. We put something somewhere... and then it's seen halfway across the room."

Mandy Allen, a waitress in the dining room at the Trustee's Office, said, "I've heard my name called quite a few times; I usually hear that on the porch. I've snuffed out a candle only to later find that it's lit again."

Seth Brewer worked with Sarah and Mandy in the dining room. Seth said that spring a tray of juice glasses fell off a table although there was nobody around the tray. He had heard of the same thing happening with a rack of plates.

A new waiter was working in the dining room. "I was training as a new employee. One night we were moving chairs from the center room. We had to clear them for the morning buffet and put them in the front sitting room. My coworker was bringing them up to me and I was hanging them on the wall. As he was getting more chairs, I came in from the hallway and I saw the rocking chair start to move by itself. I dropped the chairs, turned around and ran out of the room! I pushed the other man all the way to the back of the building and told him what happened. I wouldn't go in there by myself at night for quite a while."

Eva P. Lay worked in the kitchen of the Trustee's Office dining room. One night at about 9:30 in the evening, she left work and walked through the parking lot behind the Trustee's Office. Over in the adjacent parking lot to the west, she saw a man dressed in the old fashioned clothes of the Shaker's time including a hat. She noticed that he was not carrying a flashlight, but a <u>lantern</u>. Some of the folks in the kitchen later laughed at her and told her that it was probably one of the night security men. But the night security people don't dress up in Shaker attire and they carry flashlights, not 'old-time' lanterns.

East staircase of twin spiral staircases,
second floor, Trustee's Office

Perhaps the original Shaker Trustees still feel the need to supervise work being done in the building they constructed with their own hands. It is reported that when the men who were hired to work on the air conditioning and heating unit were in the attic crawl space, some of them have felt a tap on their shoulders. Many of the Shakertown employees have heard voices coming from 'Whitehall.' Whitehall is the back, third-floor hallway in the Trustee's Office building. It's called Whitehall because it is painted solid white. On the side of room 311 there's a service door that leads to the air conditioning units. Even when there is no one else in the building sounds of people talking will filter down from that area.

Two employees, a married couple, were cleaning the cellar of the Trustee's Office one day. They were working in separate rooms when the man suddenly saw a young girl come in. She asked him a question before she went into the room where his wife was working. But later when asked, his wife said that she had seen no one come in.

Maintenance worker 'Tucker' said that he and his coworkers would work overnight cleaning the ovens in the kitchen pots and pans room of the Trustee's Office. Tucker: "I was down in the basement of that building earlier one night to work on a pipe. Before I went back upstairs to clean the ovens, I stacked up some wooden crates to serve as a ladder to reach the pipe I was wrapping with new insulation. I returned to the kitchen and put a Janis Joplin tape on, as

18

loud as it would go. Then I heard this racket. I had watched Joyce go out the door. I <u>know</u> I was only one in the basement; everybody had left."

"When I went out to see what had caused the racket, I found every one of those milk crates knocked down throughout that passageway. I was scared to death. I felt the hair stand up on my neck. I looked around to see if someone was in the building and I found no one. I even checked the time clock just to see if someone had come in and clocked out and left. I looked in both of the bathrooms...I was totally alone in there. Then I apologized to the spirits and turned off the music and went back to work."

Tucker acknowledges that many of the sounds the village buildings make are not the sounds of restless spirits: "Pipes will moan; I've heard that."

A former employee of Pleasant Hill worked as a night security person. "It was my first evening and I was out in the village doing the rotation; checking the buildings. I was in the Trustee's Office and I went up to check on one of the security clocks. When I went up the spiral stairs and reached the top floor, I felt something breathing down the back of my neck. But there wasn't anyone there. I don't know if it was first-night jitters, a ghost or the boogie man."

Cathy Bryant of Lebanon Junction, Kentucky, and her sister Janet Robison traveled to Shakertown about five years ago. Cathy: "My husband and I had gone our first time and we enjoyed it so much. I wanted my sister to see Shakertown and to experience the food and atmosphere. We booked a night to stay together in a double room in the Trustee's Office on the third floor. Well I had a great night. We went to bed and I really didn't notice anything unusual. The next morning I got up and said, 'Janet, did you sleep well?' "

Janet answered, "No, I didn't. Between your snoring and the footsteps in the hall, I didn't get any sleep at all."

"What do you mean?" Cathy asked.

"I kept hearing footsteps. They would walk past our room...and stop. Finally, I got up the nerve to open the door and see. I thought someone was out there, prowling around. The next time I heard footsteps, I opened the door...there was nobody there. I just know that there was a ghost out there last night!"

Cathy added, "The odd thing was that we were staying in the last room at the end of the hallway, and Janet heard the footsteps come down the hallway and go past our room. There was no place to go past our room at the end of the hall--right past us was the window."

Cathy continued with another story concerning the Old Stone Shop, located a short walk westward down the village lane. "My husband passed away almost three years ago, and I wanted to revisit Pleasant Hill, because there were some good memories there for my husband and I. Janet had just laughed at the experience of the footsteps, and we had had a good time there. So my sister and I decided go back to Shakertown a couple of years later. I like to stay in the Trustee's Office, but we had called late for reservations. We were lucky to get in any building; they called us to let us know there was a cancellation. So we stayed in the Old Stone Shop on the top floor."

"When we walked in that room we got the oddest feeling. We didn't want to spend the night there. But we had reservations...So I thought, *this is crazy, we're just tired*. We unpacked and went out for a walk and returned to our room. It still felt a bit strange."

"We opened the little doors that went out to a crawl space under the eaves. There was one of those little doors by the bathroom and another door in our room. I felt a little creepy. We didn't sleep that well, although we didn't see or hear anything...it was just that <u>strange</u> feeling. I had never felt that before at Shakertown."

Walking west from the Trustee's Office one encounters a yellow, brightly painted wood building that was constructed in 1820. The Ministry's Workshop is where guests used to register for overnight stays-- the 'front desk'. This was where the ministers worked on Shaker crafts. After the initial restoration of Pleasant Hill it housed guests in two rooms on the second floor. Like the other Shaker buildings, it has wooden plank floors. The single door entrance opens into a hallway with a staircase. The hallway is flanked by two small rooms.

Ministry's Workshop

The Ministry's Workshop is oftentimes the first contact visitors have with Shakertown, as the friendly staff locate their reservations and provide a map and directions to get visitors to their accommodations. I often went directly from my drive of one to four hours to check in with the folks there and catch up a little on news and happenings in the Shaker village. I found the ladies who worked there very supportive of my intention to collect Shaker experiences.

Ruth Keller can share a few odd tales from her experience at the Ministry's Workshop. She is the front desk supervisor. Ruth has heard from upstairs the sounds of chairs being moved. Also, she was in the office with two men one time. They all heard sounds coming from the room above the front desk. At that time there were boxes stacked up in that room. The night watch man didn't go up to have a look...so she grabbed the security guard and they climbed the stairs to have a look. They found that the boxes had been thrown about! Also, the door to the room which had been left open was slammed shut.

Ruth would often hear the sound of someone walking upstairs. This happened even when the room was locked and no one was up there.

Sandy Inman, who does accounting at the Ministry's Workshop, notes that the rooms above the front desk had been guest rooms. She said that sometimes when the overnight guests had babies, the babies would wake up screaming for no apparent reason. The guests had also reported seeing rocking chairs that were rocking by themselves.

One Pleasant Hill employee stationed in the Ministry's Workshop reports that her coin container top, which had been on the verge of breaking off, was found by her to have been mysteriously returned to better condition. This happened in her own money drawer to which only she has access and must be opened with two keys.

Michelle Dunn also works at the front desk in the Ministry's Workshop. "I would always grab the railing at about the third step from the top when I came down the stairs. It seemed to be an unusual habit of mine until I heard a story from a visiting psychic. The psychic had gotten the impression that a Shaker woman had fallen from that third step." Michelle said the psychic told them the story she 'saw': "There had been a meeting upstairs of the elders and eldresses. During the meeting the elders were not in agreement and a number of people had sided with one woman. An elder was upset about this. As they were going downstairs, the man may have pushed or accidentally stepped on the woman's dress. She fell down and was seriously hurt." Michelle has heard voices in the office of the Ministry's Workshop. She reports that when she heard the voice, she turned around to see who was talking to her. She asked Chrissy, "Were you talking to me?" Chrissy replied that she hadn't been talking at all. In addition, Michelle said that the television had been turned down, so the voices weren't from the television.

Michelle Dunn saw a group of adults and children going west on the village pike in March of 1999. She had arrived to work in the Ministry's Workshop and was headed to the front door when she saw this group. But <u>this</u> group of school children were clothed in Shaker attire; the girls had dresses. Michelle smiled at the group and thought, *how quiet and orderly they are.*

It is indeed a rare sight to see a school tour at nine in the evening!

One of the closest encounters in the Ministry's Workshop and indeed in the accounts throughout the entire village is told by a new Shakertown employee who started working at the front desk. Candy worked with Michelle and told Michelle that she would very much like to see a ghost. The two walked through the village to see if they might spot a spirit gliding past on a warm spring night.

On the following night Candy and Michelle were busy working at the front desk. Candy had returned upstairs to put her receipts drawer when she rushed back downstairs. Michelle noticed that she seemed upset enough to cry and asked her, "Candy, is something wrong?"

"There's a man upstairs." Candy said aloud, and one of the security guards who were there heard that and went upstairs to investigate. Bruce Herring was serving as a night guard that night and he stated that he certainly felt a presence there. Michelle went to see if there were ghostly vibrations upstairs, but she hadn't gone halfway up the stairs when the hair on the back of her neck stood up and, she said, "My entire back felt like ice!" Michelle and the other workers believe that the ghost had walked himself down those stairs.

Unexplained sights and sounds continued the next evening when a kitchen employee, who had heard pots and pans rattling in the kitchen basement, noticed that the Ministry's Workshop back door was wide open. This happened almost immediately after

Michelle had closed and secured that same door. In addition, Candy was singled out again for a visit from the Shaker man. While Michelle was talking to someone at the back window, Candy came upon the same ghostly visitor at the front desk. He was taciturn and stared directly at her. She reports that he had a blue vest and a hat and his beard was long; his hair was brown. She will not forget his serious look.

When Candy called out, Michelle came; by then the Shaker specter had vanished.

Dolores Krier and her husband were overnight guests in the Ministry's Workshop twenty years ago. Dolores recalls that they had a choice of only two of the buildings at Pleasant Hill, since the restoration was recently undertaken. She explains that she and her husband slept on separate twin beds; the beds were very similar to the beds on which the Shakers had slept. They had a cross-woven support for mattresses filled with straw.

Dolores: "We retired for the night. I woke up about three in the morning and I felt uncomfortable... I felt a heaviness. I was lying flat on my back on the bed. When I opened my eyes I looked across the room, which wasn't very far, as the room was not big."

"I saw a series of faces appear. They showed themselves in black and white and they seemed to be male faces. Their expressions were very dour and unhappy. The faces came one after another. It was almost as if I was watching an old movie reel."

Dolores continues, "The feeling that came over me was very strong. It felt like a pressure...an anguish or misery. And it was very, very heavy-- I found it difficult to breathe. I felt so extremely uncomfortable...it was like everything within me was contracting. It was a feeling of pulling into myself."

"I turned on the light, and then the faces disappeared. But the <u>feeling</u> remained in the room. I woke my husband and I said, 'We have to leave.' It was pitch black; about three-thirty in the morning. My husband said, 'It's the middle of the night!' "

"I answered, 'But I cannot stay here. I can't stay here a moment longer. I'm finding it difficult to breathe.' So we packed our bags and we went next door, to the Trustee's Office. We told the person at the front desk we were leaving. We checked out, and it wasn't until we were in our car and driving away from Shakertown that the feeling of pressure left me."

"Since that night I have been back to Pleasant Hill for two or three visits in the last five years. I've been there as a day visitor. I have walked by the Ministry's Office where we stayed that night, but I had no strange feelings when I walked by there."

"I wonder if those vibrations, the energy of the Shakers, were more prevalent for my first visit compared to recent times; since we stayed overnight soon after the buildings were opened."

Meeting House, across from the
Centre Family Dwelling

Next to the Ministry's Workshop is the Meeting
House. The Meeting House was the spiritual center
of the village; it was where the Shakers had their
dedicated worship. Although the Shakers considered
their everyday tasks to be holy, the Meeting House
was the place where they could support each other
in the active and creative expression of their faith.
In this building they would sing and dance and
shake off their sins; the Meeting House was the site
of many of their visions and was open to visitors.
The Shakers looked to some of the inspired visitors
as possible converts to their faith.

The original meeting house was located farther
west along the village pike. It was close to where

the present craft store stands. However, during the New Madrid earthquake of 1812, that building was substantially damaged. Plans were made and executed to construct the present meeting house. The solid construction of the Meeting House is proof of the Shaker's legacy of craftsmanship and evidence of their attitude: "Do all your work as though you had a thousand years to live..."

Despite the decline of the village and the disappearance of the mortal Shakers, the restored Meeting House has survived as a wonderful and enchanting place of worship and simplicity. The Meeting House had been adapted in the 1900's as a garage (you can still see oil stains on the floor) and as a Baptist church. It was built in 1820 and had upstairs apartments for the ministry. The Meeting House is entered through two doors, separate for the men and the women. No interior columns obstructed the view or provided a hindrance for dancing and whirling. There are matching, small windows on both the men and the women's sides where the spiritual leadership observed the worshippers from the stairwells and checked for potential converts. The Meeting House is a large structure, measuring sixty by forty-four feet.

I think the Shaker singers and I, and likely many of the Pleasant Hill employees, viewed the Meeting House as the spiritual center of Shakertown. I have been built up with emotion while stomping, dancing and singing on the same floorboards that the Shakers shook up long ago. For speaking and particularly singing, the acoustics are bright and bouncy, and songs carry even outside to the village lane. I have spent many meditative moments, in morning, afternoon or evening sitting on a bench in the Meeting House, wondering if I might connect with the spirit of the Shakers. I can anytime easily close my eyes and visualize the Meeting House interior and see faces of visitors as they listen and imagine what Shaker life was truly like.

Meeting House interior, (first floor)

A visitor can find daily music and dance programs in the Meeting House. In addition, there are talks on Shaker spirituality and candlelight performances held there. Before the current Administration Building was constructed, Pleasant Hill's offices were located upstairs. Shakertown employee Ruth Keller would sometimes have to go up into those upstairs offices to turn off computer stations that had been left on. She would unlock the empty building, and two or three times, heard singing on the first floor.

Many employees have heard singing in the empty Meeting House.

Karen Preston, a former employee of Pleasant Hill, was making copies in the upstairs of the Meeting House one winter evening when the building was locked. Karen heard singing downstairs. "It was a female voice...sort of doing a scale of notes. I called Ralph to come help check it out and to meet me downstairs. At first I thought that perhaps a radio had been left on. But we found that all the offices were closed and there were no radios still on."

Another Pleasant Hill singer recently heard a ghostly voice, coming from the Meeting House. James Lochridge said, "A practice had been scheduled for the Pleasant Hill Singers for a Friday evening at 6:30, but was cancelled without me knowing about it. I arrived at the Administration building but no one was there, so I started walking to the Meeting House, the other place we usually practice, but on the way didn't see anyone else in the group, so I was starting to wonder if practice had been cancelled. As I approached the Meeting House I heard distant singing, so was glad that I'd found where we were practicing. As I neared the East side door I clearly heard the voice of a woman singing, a pentatonic scale, which the Shakers used in many of their songs, and continuing on to the front of the building past this door, the voice faded. On reaching the front I found both doors locked and nothing but silence from inside. I might have second-guessed what I heard when it seemed at a distance, but there's no question that I heard distinctly the woman's voice as I passed the side door, the pentatonic scale unmistakable. Sadly, there was no one else around at the time to confirm what I had heard."

A female employee of Shakertown who worked in accounting tells a story that perhaps reminds us of why the Shakers got their name.

"We were in the Meeting House upstairs. This was about four and a half years ago, when the offices were there. I was talking with a coworker about some of the weird things that happen at Pleasant Hill, when we noticed that the light on the wall was shaking. It was a wall sconce, and there was no reason for it to shake like that. There was nothing else in the office moving. There had been no earth tremors that day."

A former employee who worked with public relations at Pleasant Hill was also an interpreter in the Meeting House. She noted that had been about fifteen years ago.

"I had finished up a session; I'd been interpreting for a group. One woman stayed after all the other group had left. She was a charismatic who was visiting from Atlanta. She was wearing regular attire, blue jeans and a tee-shirt."

"She set her four year old daughter on a bench, and came up to me and asked if she could 'twirl'. I saw no harm in that, and the woman proceeded to spin herself, dancing, in the middle of the Meeting House. The woman spun for at least fifteen minutes without stopping. She spun with her arms out and hands upward."

"Then she suddenly stopped, without being dizzy at all. She picked up her child, thanked me and left."

Windows in Meeting House

Bill Bright, a former Pleasant Hill employee, tells of an amazing experience.

"It was in the winter of 1996, and Dixie and I were working in the village. She noticed that the candles from a candlelight performance were still in the windows of the Meeting House. Dixie decided that they needed to be put away, so we stopped in there. I helped gather up the candles and Dixie went to put them in the closet."

"Since I was a bit bored, I walked over to a spot between the two front doors to sing a little. I was next to a gap in the wall benches, facing the back wall. I started to sing sets of three, descending notes (triads). Since I had spent plenty of time in high school band, I figured that it'd be a neat exercise to try the acoustics in the large room of the Meeting House."

"As I was singing, something appeared in the middle of the benches to my right, on the sister's side. For lack of a better explanation, it looked like a human form, very similar to the special effect done in Star Trek when they beam up somebody. It seemed to rise up from the floor to my height. At that point, the hair on the right side of my body stood on end, while the left side was not affected. I immediately got cold chills, like I had just walked into a meat locker. I just wanted to get out of there. I left the building immediately, quickly enough to make Dixie come out after me."

"She asked me, 'What's wrong?'"

"I told her what had happened and she suggested that I talk to Randy Folger, the music director. When I saw Randy, I told him about the experience and he simply asked me if I knew what I had been doing. At that point I had no idea. Then Randy asked me to sing as I had been singing in the Meeting House. After I sang for him, Randy explained to me that I had unwittingly been singing the 'Angel Shout'. The Angel Shout was a set of notes that were sung like: 'Lo...lo...lo...' and were sung in descending thirds. The Angel Shout was supposed to call the Shakers to meeting."

"Today I have no reservations about going into the Meeting House, but I will not try my experiment again!"

Outside the Meeting House, on the village road, there have been a few sightings. The village pike was actually US Highway 68 until the creators of the restored Shakertown wisely diverted the highway farther south. It is now a peaceful village lane lined by trees. Visitors find Pleasant Hill employees demonstrating crafts in the shade of the trees. Soldiers from the biannual Civil War encampment march down the pike, much like the traveling armies of the Union and Confederate forces did in the nineteenth century. Visitors ride horse-drawn wagons on their Shakertown tour. It is common to see the Pleasant Hill employees, dressed in Shaker attire, walking to work or back from lunch.

When I visit Pleasant Hill, I love to walk down the village lane. From the walking road that leads from the parking lot, past the gift shop, I quickly get to the heart of the village. A glance east or westward down the village pike gives me a rapid assessment of how many visitors are about that day and what kind of demonstrations are happening. I've enjoyed the peaceful pike in all kinds of weather, and it's pleasant to stroll down the lane and look at the marvelous Shaker buildings, or, to view the lane from inside one of the wavy glass antique windows.

Randy Folger, the music director for ten years, was everyone's dear friend and he inspired many a visitor with his sweet voice and kind eyes. Randy provided me with a number of the Shaker ghost stories and he was interested in the unusual happenings. Since I began gathering the Shaker ghost stories, Randy, and a number of other Pleasant Hill interpreters, have passed on. (See Memoriam in the back of this book.)

Randy Folger told of an interesting event that occurred during the 1996 Civil War reenactment. He said that many of men who were portraying the soldiers knew very little about the Shakers and their type of worship. They had placed an overnight sentry at the corner of the Centre Family Dwelling, across from the Meeting House. Susan Lyons Hughes, the Education Specialist, checked on them the next day. Randy said, "These guys were terrified!"

The sentries asked, "What the heck was going on last night? At three in the morning we heard the most awful racket coming from the Meeting House. We heard people clapping their hands and singing; they were stomping and shouting too!" Randy said that they were very serious about the truth of their experience. "They discovered how the Shakers worshipped."

The former waiter (who told of the rocking chair that moved) heard from some of the Civil War reenactors too. He stated that two soldiers told him that they were in front of the Meeting House one night. They saw two figures approaching from the west end of the pike. The figures were carrying lanterns and were dressed in Shaker clothes. But when they got closer to the reenactors...they disappeared.

"Another man was walking down the street in front of the Trustee's Office. He saw someone go by him who was dressed in Shaker attire. He figured it was Randy Folger, and he wondered why Randy didn't greet him. As he thought that, the employee turned around to discover that the figure had vanished."

Interpreters walking
(westward) down village lane

A former Pleasant Hill housekeeper told of a couple of guests who were walking down the village pike one evening. They reported that a man, dressed in Shaker garb, was walking toward them. The couple were walking from the Trustee's Office toward the West Family Dwelling. As they approached the man and prepared to speak...the man simply disappeared! The couple reported being firm disbelievers in ghosts <u>before</u> this incident.

One overnight guest to Pleasant Hill saw a disappearing figure walk across the village pike. When I was visiting Pleasant Hill to perform a Christmas program with the singers, Bob Woodruff was excited to tell me his story. He had made many trips to Shakertown, and had heard of the Shaker ghosts but hadn't really ever expected that he would have one himself. "On the evening of December 11th, 1998, I was walking west on the village road. There was an overcast sky and no wind. It seemed like rain was about to fall and it was a little cold. There was no one else about and it was <u>very</u> quiet."

"As I came up to the Trustee's Office building, by the little turnaround drive, I saw a woman cross the village road farther down. She walked from the Meeting House to the Centre Family Dwelling. She looked like a Shaker. She had a long, blue dress with a white apron and a white bonnet. I even noticed the bonnet details: the bonnet was of solid material with a wide brim across the front and sides; it completely covered her hair in back. The wide side brim shielded her face from my view. The white bonnet and apron stood out in the dim light."

Bob: "She passed right next to the lamp post, going from the eastern gate outside the Meeting House to the matching gate directly across the lane in front of the Centre Family Dwelling. It seemed that her hands were in her pockets. Since I had just an hour previously arrived from California, I was tired and thought no more that she must have been a docent working there. I looked away from her for a few moments; when I looked back she was gone."

"I assumed that she had gone into the building, or perhaps around the other side of the Centre Family Dwelling. I was curious. When I reached the building, I circled completely around it and listened for her. I looked for her white clothing in the darkness but the Centre Family Dwelling was dark and the doors were locked and there was no one to be found."

"It was only then that I realized what had happened, and I felt very fortunate. While I have had more dramatic 'encounters' at my home, this was my first experience at Shakertown."

Centre Family Dwelling

The very large Centre Family Dwelling dominates the central village at Pleasant Hill. It stands across the village road from the Meeting House. The two buildings provide a historical focal point and visitors are often found in either building or standing on the pike between the two. The Centre Family Dwelling took ten years to be completed (1834), and is an architectural marvel, inside and out. Large white limestone blocks provide sturdy walls. The inside is spacious and inspiring with its tall ceilings and broad hallway. Just inside the entrance, historical interpreters greet the visitors. They patiently explain building features, exhibits and Shaker customs. Some of the rooms display Shaker industries: seed packaging, cider-making, weaving. There are other rooms with separate brethren's and sister's beds, some with small linen bags strung on the bedposts. The bags have herbs to repel insects.

The Centre Family Dwelling has three floors exhibiting exquisite Shaker craftsmanship in architectural detail and exhibits. A large bell on the roof of the ell is rung by the interpreters to call visitors to the Meeting House for music programs.

When I sing at Shakertown, I usually have and take the opportunity to go into the Centre Family Dwelling. I would wander throughout the building and try and locate one of my favorite cats who is often found inside the Centre Family Dwelling or outside on the limestone steps. I feel like my visit is complete if I've had a chance to pet Mischief, the tortoise shell tabby cat.

She who knows?—"Mischief"

Carol Zahn, an interpreter who worked in the Centre Family Dwelling, said that she and the other interpreters have heard singing there. "A number of times, when we're closing up the Centre Family Dwelling at 5:30 or six, we have heard the soft sound of an older woman singing. This has come from the upstairs meeting room. I am not surprised that there are Shaker spirits in residence here. The Shakers believed their spirits stayed here until Judgment Day." Carol is a dear friend and Shaker singer who passed on; she loved to hear about the Shaker ghost stories, and she and her daughter had a few of their own stories from their home.

Another Centre Family Dwelling interpreter says, "I've gotten a weird feeling when I'm upstairs in the infirmary exhibit. And an odd thing happened once when I was cleaning out spider webs in the loom room. I had cleaned out the spider webs in all the other rooms without any problem. But when I came back into the loom room after about five minutes, there was a whole new batch of spider webs there."

Interpreter Mrs. Mary Lee Woford had guided visitors through the Centre Family Dwelling for many years. She had been a Shakertown employee for 24 years. Mrs. Woford would often be seen standing near the entranceway to the interpreter's tiny office/ closet as she waited for the next group of inquiring souls to enter the Centre Family Dwelling. A number of her fellow interpreters noticed something interesting on the one year anniversary of her passing away, (1998). The lovely and strong scent of lilacs could be smelled right at her favorite spot.

Gill Lay worked in maintenance at Shakertown for eighteen years. He had an odd encounter in the Centre Family Dwelling when he was working there one winter evening around 5:30. It was dark and he had set up three or four lamps on the first floor in order to be able to see to mop the entire floor. He recalls that it took about an hour to mop the floor prior to waxing it the following day.

"I had of course locked the outside door of the Centre Family Dwelling. I finished mopping and went upstairs to use the third floor bathroom. When I was up there I heard footsteps downstairs. I hollered, 'what are you doing down there?' "

"Nobody answered; nobody was down there or in the building with me. I asked the other night worker and he hadn't been to or in the Centre Family Dwelling at all."

Beverly Rogers has worked at Shakertown for over a decade. She can be found in the Centre Family Dwelling with other experienced and talented interpreters.

"We were having a performance for the Friends of Pleasant Hill Forum. We always had it on the second floor of the Centre Family Dwelling in the meeting room." (Not to be confused with the Meeting House which is across the village pike from the Centre Family Dwelling.)

"One of our administration employees had been in the brother's room, the first room on the right, when you enter the building. She came out, scared to death, and said, 'I'll not come back in this building at night.' "

"I asked her, 'What happened?' "

"She said, 'I had a cold breeze blow up my dress!' "

The Farm Deacon's Shop is located close to the Centre Family Dwelling and it was the original Centre Family Dwelling. It is the oldest permanent structure at Pleasant Hill and was built in 1809. It is a two-story stone structure and is a short walk west from the Centre Family Dwelling. There are a few stories of ghosts from folks who have worked in the Farm Deacon's Shop; some of those stories will come later in this book. Here is one story related by interpreter Carol Zahn.

Farm Deacon's Shop

"I've felt or seen a number of strange things at the Farm Deacon's Shop. The Shakers had used the building for a number of purposes: family dwelling, tavern, shop and residence for the farm deacons. Some of us interpreters working there have heard footsteps upstairs, and the creaking sounds of boards being walked on, up and down the staircase."

Carol: "Some of the interpreters have smelled lilacs there. Also, some workers have felt an oppressive male presence in the Farm Deacon's Shop. Oftentimes, we've noticed strange things happening when the village was almost vacant, during the time when the majority of tourists were gone."

"I was alone one time, in the Farm Deacon's Shop, when I got the feeling that someone was watching me. I sensed that someone was outside, near the window, next to where I was sitting. I felt the hair stand up on the back of my neck, and I had a cold feeling come into my body. I heard the sound of walking in the cellar below; and I felt that someone was <u>in</u> the cellar, looking up at me through the cracks in the floorboards."

"I was so scared that I couldn't talk. I couldn't wait until the twenty minutes were over when I could close up and go. I couldn't get out of there fast enough. I had the overwhelming feeling that there was something there I didn't want to see!"

Near the intersection of the east/west village pike and the north/south village lane is the Carpenter's Shop. The Carpenter's Shop is located diagonally across the intersection from the Farm Deacon's Shop. The Carpenter's Shop is a brick building constructed in 1815. It was used as a blacksmith and wagon shop until 1843. It was rebuilt in 1870 for the manufacture of brooms. The Carpenter's Shop is currently the Pleasant Hill Craft Store. The Craft Store is a well-frequented building for many a visitor at Pleasant Hill. Each time I go to a Shaker singing performance, I like to take a fellow singer and walk down the village lane or the parallel orchard road to the Craft Store. It's warm in winter, and cool in summer and we can easily spend our one-hour breaks between performances there. There are books, candles, woodwork, musical tapes, and Shaker-reproduction swallow tail boxes. I've both shopped at the Craft Store in both fantasy and parting with real money.

Rose Sorrell, the co-owner of the Harrodsburg Bakery, started working at Shakertown when she was fifteen years old. She worked in the gift shop, which was first housed in the Farm Deacon's Shop. After she'd worked there for two years, the gift shop was moved to its present location in the Carpenter's Shop.

"Early on, in the new building, I noticed a man's voice. It was a gentle voice. I only seemed to notice it when I was getting ready to lock up and leave. I'd say that I heard that voice about once a month, and only when I was right at the door. I didn't tell anyone else about the voice because I thought I was the only one who heard it."

"Well, one time I was again at the door, but with a coworker. We both heard the voice simultaneously! We looked at each other, and I asked her, 'Did you hear that voice?' "

She said, "Yes!" That's when they both admitted to hearing the voice. The other worker said that she wasn't sure if it was a voice or a noise, and if it was telling them to get out or to stay.

Carpenter's Shop

On another occasion Rose and Amy Inman McGinnis, and some other workers, were in the Craft Store downstairs, in the break room. They were at the kitchen table, when Amy said she heard the sound of running water. She heard this sound <u>over</u> the noise of the television that was turned on. They looked and found that the water was running full stream. They turned off the water, but several minutes later the running water was again heard. They never had any other problems with that water faucet, before or since that time.

Continuing with our ghost tour; imagine again walking west and across the village pike to the next Shaker building. This is the Old Stone Shop which the Shakers made in 1811. This was a West Family dwelling and later became the village medical office. There are now rooms for overnight guests. If you stay in one particular upstairs room there, you can find an undated poem that is written in pencil on the stucco wall. The poem is in room 174 and is located near a window. The restorers kindly left a frame around the writing, leaving the poem intact with new stucco all around it. One could imagine a woman, having given up the fullness of marriage, writing this heartfelt remembrance:

> Dost ever thou think
> O Darling fair loved one
> of the first time we stood linked
> in each other's embrace
> Dost think as thou goest on the way
> of that time when my heart
> was so full with love overflowing
> That I spoke not but kissed thee
> and sent thee away

As I read this intimate note, I tried to imagine what life was like for young women in the nineteenth century, and how their choice might be limited to being a homemaker. But suppose your husband was killed in the War Between the States, and your land and home were legally given to another male relative or in-law. Sacrificing love and property to join the Shakers might be a wise choice. The Shakers gave their children a fine education, and hard work was done by all but the very rich anyway. But it did tug at my heart to read these lines of lost love.

Old Stone Shop

Susan Hughes stayed in the Old Stone Shop one night. She had been working at Shakertown during the weekend of the funeral reenactment. It was late at night and she was tired. As she went into the Old Stone Shop to prepare for the night she announced out loud to the spirits that she wanted to sleep. She told the spirits that she wasn't in the mood for any of their visits.

She tried to sleep, but she kept feeling like a feather was being pulled across her nose. After about an hour or so, she turned on the light. She said aloud, "I'm sorry, I didn't mean to offend you." Then she found that she went to sleep without further incident.

I found one humorous ghost story from the Old Ministry's Shop. This is a wood building that is a little northeast of the Old Stone Shop. It was built about 1812 and had a variety of uses, including service as a school house at one time.

One of the Confederate reenactors, Stephen Bowling was giving tours of the Civil War encampment. I chatted with the reenactors about their camping weekend, and I eventually got around to asking them about Shaker ghosts. I figured that they were rugged kind of guys who probably looked at life realistically, and that they likely didn't believe in ghosts. But the reenactors immediately spoke up about something that had happened that weekend. They had been in the Old Ministry's Shop. They had closed the back door, but they found it kept popping open. The men would yell, "Come on in!" Then they'd get up and shut the door. This happened four times. Perhaps the ghost of a Shaker schoolboy was finally able to play some pranks without facing the teacher's punishment.

Across a wide lawn space, (where the Civil War reenactors camp), from the Old Ministry's Shop, is the West Family Sister's Shop. The West Family Sister's Shop was constructed thirty-two years after the Old Ministry's Shop was built. The Shaker women, as productive and industrious as the Shaker brethren, pressed and packaged medicinal herbs. They also made carpeting and corn shuck mattresses.

West Family Sister's Shop

Guests from Louisville, Mary Hand and her husband stayed in the West Family Sister's Shop about four years ago. Mary thought they came in the fall, as she remembered it being cool and they used the fireplace.

"My husband had a lumpy bed and we got him on a different bed in an adjacent room. I kept hearing footsteps throughout the night. They seemed to be going to the bathroom; I thought that my husband must have had diarrhea. I felt sorry for him because I heard the footsteps going all night."

"About three in the morning I again awoke to hear footsteps going to the bathroom. I decided to check on him and make sure that he was all right. I waited and waited outside the closed bathroom door. After a long time, I knocked and then looked into the bathroom to discover that nobody was there. I looked down the hallway and I could see my husband sleeping in his bed."

Mary finished her tale: "I was sleepy and confused and I once again went back to sleep...still hearing footsteps. This time they were coming up the steps. I was a bit concerned, and I looked out to check for an intruder. Once again there was no one there. I fell asleep and dreamt that I was telling my friends that I had spent the night at Shakertown, with ghosts."

"I asked my husband in the morning if he had been up to use the bathroom. He said that he had slept soundly; he hadn't used the bathroom all night!"

Rose Sorrell remembers some customers who came into the craft shop where she worked. They had stayed overnight in the West Family Sister's Shop. The man said that he was awakened from his sleep by hands that were shaking him. He said that when he looked about, he saw that his wife was fast asleep.

A few other buildings close to the West Family Sister's Shop which also carry some good ghost tales are the West Family Wash House and the West Family Dwelling.

The West Family Wash House sits almost next to the West Family Sister's Shop, separated only by a small building, the Preserve Shop. The Wash House was built in 1842.

Bruce Herring, the riverboat captain, relates a story told to him by Marty Gray. He said that Marty was checking up on things in the West village. He decided to walk instead of drive the night security truck. He looked up into the windows of the West Family Wash House and he saw someone inside who was standing by one of the windows. He went into the Wash House and looked all around but discovered no one inside.

One of the Civil War reenactors previously worked during the night security shift at Pleasant Hill. "I would get eerie feelings, and the hair on the back of my neck would stand up. I remember getting those feelings in the West Family Wash House and in the West Family Dwelling when I was upstairs. I felt like I was being watched. I get that same feeling when I go into my grandmother's house, which is supposed to be haunted."

West Family Dwelling

The next and last building in the tour of village haunts is the West Family Dwelling. The West Family Dwelling was constructed in 1821. The older Shakers lived here and were assigned duties requiring less strenuous labor. It's a large structure with a brick front facing the village pike; the cool basement cellar served as a morgue in the Shaker's time. The West Family Dwelling is close to the other West village buildings; they're grouped at the west end of the turnpike and are the last historic buildings one sees on the way to the graveyard. The Shaker singers sometime have stayed overnight in the West Family Dwelling during our retreats. And we often eat our lunch before a warm weather performance, down in the basement summer kitchen.

Stephen Bowling and his fellow reenactors from the 4th Kentucky Volunteer Infantry had a Shaker experience there. Stephen said, "Two years ago we held our Civil War encampment. We were driven into the West Family Dwelling to spend the night because of rain. We were upstairs and in the back room. Well, the men couldn't find a switch to turn off the lights." (The light bulbs are in reproduction wooden wall sconces.) "The guys unscrewed all the bulbs so we'd be able to sleep better without the lights being on."

"One light bulb came on, so they unscrewed it again. Then <u>two</u> bulbs came on and they got up and unscrewed those again. They actually then took out those two bulbs, completely removing them from their sockets. Then another one came on! In the course of an hour, four bulbs came on, just as quickly as they could get them unscrewed. And the door to the restroom swung open as they unscrewed the last light bulb."

There are rooms for overnight lodging in the West Family Dwelling. In addition, there are larger meeting rooms, and in the basement cellar, a lovely summer/winter kitchen.

Marty Gray and another maintenance worker were called over to the West Family Dwelling. A guest in a room on the first floor had reported hearing the sound of scratching on the door. Arrangements were made for the guest to switch to another room. Then Marty and his coworker spent the night in the guest's room, waiting to see if perhaps a raccoon had gotten into the building.

After a while, they heard the scratching sounds too. When they turned on the lights and looked at the door, they were surprised to find scratch marks on the <u>inside</u> of the door!

One employee started out working for Shakertown in the summer kitchen as a waitress. It is a long dining area, with wooden octagonal supporting pillars. There are large whitewashed stones that make up its walls. A waiter reported that the new waitress was working in the north room of the summer kitchen.

"She was serving vegetables and passing by a table of two patrons, when she felt somebody jab an elbow into her side. She almost dropped the vegetables. She thought that it was Michelle or one of the other girls who hit her by accident."

"She went back into the kitchen and asked her fellow workers, 'Which one of you all bumped into me? You almost made me spill a bowlful on those people.'"

"And they all said, 'We've been back here!' The waitress couldn't explain what happened."

Leona Inman, who works at the front desk, tells of housekeeping workers who were at the West Family Dwelling. They had cleaned a room and then locked it. Later, they heard the sound of furniture being moved in the same room. When they unlocked the room to have a look, they found that all the furniture had been moved to the middle of the room.

Richard Word of Buckhorn, Kentucky, stayed in the West Family Dwelling.

"It was October of 1993, my wife and I and our two and a half year old daughter had gone to Shakertown to meet with my brother in law and his wife. They had gotten married there about seven months before and they had wanted to come back. We stayed in a house that had four separate living areas, each one consisting of a bedroom with a sitting parlor, and a main parlor downstairs. As we were checking in we got word from them that they were going to be late. They were supposed to be there at four in the afternoon; we got there at five. (They had told us they'd be there about eight.) About seven o'clock we were sitting down in the parlor waiting for them to drive up."

"We heard a door open upstairs. We heard footsteps along the upstairs hall. Then we heard the footsteps coming downstairs, through the hallway and going out the front door. But the door never opened and there was no one on the stairs."

"My wife and I were thinking, *We're going to get out of here now.* Our daughter made the comment, 'Well it's okay, he just wants us to know that he's going to take care of us.' And so we stayed there and in about twenty minutes Tom and Andrea came. We haven't yet told this story to anyone because we didn't think anyone would believe us, but that's what happened!"

Another incident which occurred in the West Family Dwelling was told to me by the employees of Shakertown. An overnight guest reported that a woman dressed as a Shaker knocked on her door at five in the morning. This out-of-state guest had stayed at Shakertown many times. She works for a hospice and was visiting Pleasant Hill with her mother. The Shaker-dressed female used a key to enter the room after knocking, and she carried a stack of fresh towels. The guest expressed surprise at receiving this housekeeping call so early, and the Shaker woman reportedly replied that it was a courtesy extended to them. The guest then asked that she at least please be quiet so as to not awaken her mother.

In the morning, the woman noticed that the towel which she had used to wipe off her makeup was either gone or had indeed been cleaned by the Shaker woman. Later that morning the guest inquired about the unusual timing of her "room service". She was accurately informed that the housekeeping staff wear a simple service uniform which does not resemble the period Shaker clothing. In addition, housekeepers report for duty at an hour more convenient for most mortals.

Finally, the female guest stated that the Shaker ghost had been running the clothes washer and dryer, located below her guest room, all night.

It seems that the Shaker spirits are as dedicated to helpful service in their new lives as they were when they assisted each other and "the world" as mortals.

Two stories from two other sites are fascinating to hear. The West Lot Dwelling is west of the village proper and takes a short drive of one and one-half miles to reach. The drive is beautiful and takes the visitor over Shawnee Run Creek. The West Lot Dwelling is an impressive limestone building which stands on high ground and overlooks rolling hills. This building was occupied by those persons who were not yet fully Shakers; they had not signed a covenant of full commitment to the Society of Believers. Shakertown employee Dave Brown relates a puzzling experience from the West Lot Dwelling.

"I've worked at Pleasant Hill for five years and I'm currently the front desk supervisor. My first job, though, was in meeting services. We would set up and take down the meeting rooms. The West Lot Dwelling is the primary conference area for the village."

West Lot Dwelling

"We had two meetings going on down at the West Lot. One night while working late after a particular group had left, I was cleaning the upstairs room while waiting for the downstairs group to finish. It was probably 8:30 or nine o'clock on a winter evening, so it was fully dark. I had cleaned the upstairs room and I had some electronic equipment that was still out, so I dead bolted the two interior doors from the inside and went out the side door and locked it behind me with my key."

"By this time the other group had left, so I went downstairs and started clearing the coffee pots and cleaning up. That's when I heard the footsteps. I was in the basement and heard the sound of footsteps walking from one end to the other on the first floor. I didn't really give it too much thought at the time, because we have people walking around these buildings all the time. But I got to thinking; *maybe I better go up and check.* When I went up I found the two interior doors were still bolted from the inside and the upstairs door that I had exited was still locked. I thought that maybe one of the maintenance guys had been over to check in with me. I called the front desk to ask if there was anyone staying in the building that night. They told me that no one was staying there. Then I talked to the maintenance man, who was on duty, and he said, 'No, I wasn't down there; I had no reason to be there.' "

Dave continued: "It struck me as weird because the sounds of the footsteps were very distinct. I heard them not once, but walking back and forth. There are all sorts of funny things out here. You'll catch things out of the corner of your eye. It's not anything that you can put a finger on, but you'll see little glimpses of things. A couple of times I've had an eerie feeling, like someone's looking at me. The hair on the back of my neck will stand up and I'll just know that a ghost is there. I recognize that feeling from a haunted apartment my ex-wife and I had in California."

Pleasant Hill Cemetery

No account of a haunted village would be complete without a tale from the graveyard! The Shakers' cemetery is located one-fourth mile west, along the village turnpike. It is a peaceful site on a small knoll with tall evergreens and cedar trees. As it has been restored, there is now a neat, white wooden plank fence surrounding it. When I visited Shakertown, coming for the singing performances, I had walked to the graveyard and stood outside the wooden fence. I wondered if the Shaker spirits were present there, but I really didn't feel anything. Also, I didn't hear any stories during 1998 and 1999 when I gathered the majority of the ghost stories. I was a little disappointed that such an exciting village for spirit activity had no ghost story from the graveyard. But eventually I was given the name of a man who, it was suggested, had an intense tale to relate. I am grateful that he shared it with me...

Thirty-two years ago, before the restoration of Pleasant Hill, the graveyard was a wild and wonderful place for young boys to explore. Twin brothers who lived near Shakertown set out with one of their buddies on a summer day, looking for a bit of adventure. The twins were twelve years old and their companion was ten years old. Their friend seemed to be one of those boys whose adventures often got him into trouble. They walked over the 'kissing bridge' and past the ruins of the Shaker grist mill. On other days they might have played in the creek or crawled up the mill's dried-out aqueduct.

The trio went east along the old pike, traveling the same historic road on which stagecoaches had driven. They headed over to a favorite pond and checked out frogs and fishes. But the pond wasn't too exciting; they'd fished there for a number of years. So they wandered over to the rough place that had once been the Shaker graveyard. The smaller and nameless markers had long been grown over. Only a few and taller headstones were visible, and three boys with blue jeans had to scuffle past thorny locust to find those gravestones. Through a small jungle of vines and honeysuckle, the youths crawled into a small clearing by a tree and found a few headstones waiting for their inspection.

One of the twins figured out that they could scoop up some dirt and use it to try to rub off the thick moss from the marble. They worked on the headstone, removing some moss and trying to read letters and numbers that would tell the story of a deceased Shaker. After they had satisfied their curiosity, the younger lad suddenly decided to push the gravestone over; it fell with a <u>thud</u> into the weeds. The twins sensed that even boyish pranks and juvenile experimenting has its limits, and they worked to right the heavy stone while the prankster watched. After some trying, the third boy felt guilty and he lent his help to the efforts to lift the stone. As hard as they tried, though, the three boys simply could not bring the Shaker monument to its original spot.

The boys walked about twenty feet over to the only other visible headstone still standing, to have a look at it. It tilted slightly and had less moss on it. As they were examining the second stone, one of the twins looked back at the first gravestone; it had come back up, by itself, to its original position! The boys all stared at the self-risen marble monument for a moment, in shock and disbelief. They then escaped from the brambles at a speed greater than their entrance, scared to death of the power of the unknown.

Only recently have the twins, now in their mid-forties, been willing to return to look for the self-rising tombstone. The third boy can be found in the state penitentiary. The twins <u>have</u> located that same pair of gravestones. Perhaps thirty-two years ago a guardian Shaker spirit was simply offering kind help to the boys who couldn't fix their mistake.

Dixie Huffman, Beverly Rogers and Randy Folger

CHAPTER 3

A Whirlwind

I made wonderful new friends when I joined the Shaker singers. Three of those new friends were Dixie, Beverly, and Randy. All of them had been working at Shakertown for many years and each one seemed very dedicated to serving the public while dressed as Shakers. Beverly and Dixie were interpreters and Randy was the musical director. The Pleasant Hill interpreters are tireless workers who, for minimum pay, patiently explain Shaker lore to hundreds and thousands of visitors. They wear reproduction, Shaker clothing. They bake bread and pies in the

Shaker, brick-lined ovens. They sing and dance and speak of Shaker beliefs. They explain exhibits and clarify the Shaker world view, usually while standing on tired feet. They represent not only Shakertown but also the Shakers themselves. Some visitors believe that the interpreters are current day Shakers. The interpreters are the next best thing to traveling back in time for those who come and want to know more about these dedicated and spiritual folk.

Randy, Beverly and Dixie were all Pleasant Hill Singers, and employees. And being around the village so much, they had a number of Shaker ghost stories to share. I interviewed Beverly and Dixie at Shakertown. I visited Randy Folger at his nearby home and recorded our interview on cassette, though some of his best stories came when we were later walking with no tape recorder. Here are the stories of who they are and what they saw and heard.

Dixie Huffman   photo by Don Pelly

Dixie Huffman

"I was born in a house that is on land once owned by the Shakers, just down the road a little. I taught school for 31 years, second through fourth grade, in Mercer County. At that time I was teaching in the largest elementary school in the state under one roof, with over 1100 students. I did enjoy the teaching. A few years ago, the frame building that had been next to my family home was torn down. That was a public school named Shakertown Elementary, and my mother had taught school there. When I was two, we moved over to a tenant building on what was the Shaker's West lot area. At the age of six, we moved to Harrodsburg; it had been too far for me to walk to school. The Woodard family had bought the West

Lot land in 1917, and kept it until the mid-eighties, when it was sold to the Pleasant Hill Corporation."

"I was raised in the Southern Baptist Church; I've belonged to the same church since I was nine years old. I have a brother who lives in Tennessee, and I have a sister, Betty Jo, who also works at Shakertown as an interpreter. I have three daughters, six grandchildren, and three great-grandchildren. They occasionally like to come to Shakertown."

"I started at Pleasant Hill in 1971 working weekends and summer months. Then I retired from teaching in 1979 and became a full-time employee; it's been 29 years. Back then the season started in the middle of March and went to the last of November. I didn't work as many days in the winter; sometimes, I would come for the winter weekends. I really enjoy being here; I enjoy the people that we see. I like the atmosphere. Whenever you come into a Shaker village you find a sense of peace and quiet and well-being. You leave the entire outside world behind."
I liked Dixie because she had an even keeled temperament; she seemed very straightforward yet at the same time quite kind. Dixie was one of the local Mercer County inhabitants who'd been there a long time. I bet she had many more stories not even in the ghost category.

Dixie said that she has smelled the strong, sweet scent of lilacs under the stairway in the cellar of the Centre Family Dwelling. She says that she and Beverly were both walking down the turnpike one day, when they simultaneously looked at each other, smelling a strong lavender scent...and then the perfume was gone.

Dixie reports that spirit-people have been seen sitting at the loom upstairs. As Dixie headed out of the Centre Family Dwelling at closing time one day, she looked up and saw a woman in a green dress that was looking down the stairs.

Dixie describes her sister, Betty Jo Peavler, as a 'no nonsense' person. She said that one day Betty Jo left the Centre Family Dwelling, and walked across the village road to do a tour in the Meeting House. She unlocked a side door, and then went over to one of the front doors to open it for the public. The door was unlocked but she could not pull it open. There was no reason for it not to open. Betty Jo asked a man on the other side of the door, outside, to pull hard to open the door. He did and he went flying backwards. The man wondered what was wrong with Betty Jo.

One Halloween, Dixie experienced some unusual events. She was in the Centre Family Dwelling when she went upstairs to use the bathroom. She heard the toilet flushing, and she thought that it might be someone in the adjoining restroom. But as she looked at the toilet right in front of her she saw that an invisible someone had pulled the toilet handle.

Dixie reported that a couple who had recently stayed in the East Family Brethren's Shop on the second floor told her that they heard strange sounds from the attic. It sounded like someone turning over in or moving a bed. The 'bedsprings' were creaking; and it went on for some time.

On Halloween, Dixie and Ella Garrison were working as interpreters in the Farm Deacon's Shop. The wooden barrier gate inside the shop started rattling, and wouldn't stop. This went on all day. Dixie and Ella checked the furnace to see if it was causing the rattling. They tried bouncing on the wooden floorboards, but they couldn't make the gate rattle. She says that the gate never rattled again.

I was finishing the research for this book and went around the village to obtain signed releases for the use of people's names in the book. During that trip I received yet more stories. Dixie related another fascinating tale.

"One night there was going to be a program of Shaker music in the Meeting House presented by the Pleasant Hill Singers; this was before I joined the Singers. I liked to come over and hear them on Saturday nights. They were singing for a group from the Friends of Pleasant Hill. I was standing in front of the Meeting House as I was waiting for the program to start."

"I looked over to the Centre Family Dwelling and I saw the most brilliant light in the transom and around the door. I thought, *what in the world is causing that?* I stood there and looked at it for a while...and it went off. It just stopped. And I didn't think about telling anyone else until we got through singing. Then I told Randy Folger (the music director) what I had seen."

"We decided that we'd better go over and check the doors and the windows; this was before we had the alarm system. The light looked like it might be coming from the cellar. It was a bright, reddish-orange. We came over and checked all the windows and all the doors, but nothing was open. Then we went over to the front desk and I asked the girl who was working there, 'Has anybody been over to the Centre Family Dwelling?' She said, 'No, no one's been there; no one has checked out the key.' I told them what had happened and they didn't know what to make of it, either. No one had been in the Centre Family Dwelling; no one could have gotten in there, and I'm the only one who saw the light. Although there had been other people standing there, I had never thought to ask them if they saw it too. It was the strangest looking bright red-orange light, maybe like a glow. I never figured out where it came from. And I've stood over there at night and many other times, and that's the only time I saw that light."

Beverly Rogers

"I've been in Kentucky since 1973. I am originally from New Jersey. When we moved to Florida I did not work, because we had children who were growing up. When my youngest child went to school I started working at Pleasant Hill. That's when I really became involved with the Shakers and their history. I've always been an interpreter. I volunteered some time during the winters; sometimes I did journal research. This is my 13th year as an employee of Shakertown. I sing with the Pleasant Hill Singers and I love it! I live nearby, in Harrodsburg."

"I was in the Farm Deacon's Shop; it was late afternoon, in October. There was a thunderstorm; it was about five in the afternoon and it was very dark, very dreary in the building. I heard something upstairs fall. At that time, you could go through the doors and go upstairs. I went upstairs and went through the guest rooms to see what had fallen. But there was nothing that could have fallen; there was nothing I found on the floor. So I went back downstairs and sat on the chair...I heard it again! I thought, *Maybe there's a loose shutter or something on the third floor.* So I went up to the second floor and halfway up to the third floor and I thought-*What in the world am I doing up here?* I ran down the steps, three at a time. I <u>still</u> didn't see anything that had fallen down. I got down to the first floor door, shut it and locked it. And then I caught my breath, panting, after rushing downstairs. I felt like I was blocking 'it' out, whatever had dropped this thing up there."

"When I went home, my son said, 'Mom, if it was a ghost, he could have gone right through you.' And I said, 'No, they would not have done that. Because then they would have had <u>my</u> spirit, living in that building with the Shaker spirit, and they <u>never</u> would have put up with that!'

That really did scare me and I called Dixie. I guess I was scared, also, because it was so dark, and there was thunder outside. Whatever it was that fell, I have never found it."

What attracted me about Beverly was her spunk, and I also got the feeling that here was someone that would stand by you, thick and thin. I felt a bit insecure when I joined the Shaker singers, not the least reason being that I didn't know how to read music. I also didn't belong to the Mercer County locals nor was I even a Kentucky native. But interacting with Beverly, I felt that it really didn't matter. We were there to have fun and learn, and she was always happy to see me!

For many years, Beverly worked weekends in the Meeting House, where she sat in a little room adjacent to the large meeting room, waiting for the visitors. As she sat there with the door partially open, sometimes she would hear singing. She'd look out into the Meeting House and no one would be there. One day Dixie came in and asked her about the music director, Randy Folger. "Where's Randy?" "Well," Beverly said, "he left a while ago."

Dixie replied, "He did not, because I heard him singing in here."

Beverly relates another story. "About two years ago, a woman and her eight year old child were touring the Centre Family Dwelling. The lady and her little boy came downstairs and said that they had been in the loom room. She asked us if we had seen or heard anything there before. Then she described how they had seen the apron on the bonnet (the fabric attached to the straw bonnet to keep the sun off a person's neck) moving back and forth."

" 'But,' the visitor said, 'there was no breeze in that room.' "

Beverly then told me, "Of course, there couldn't have possibly been a breeze in the room. We don't keep those windows open because we aren't up there very much. And we are supposed to keep the windows down because the windows have ultraviolet blocking."

"We've seen several things in that room before. I feel it's one of the rooms that are very active."

As part of her duties, Beverly would often unlock and prepare the Meeting House prior to a special performance.

Beverly: "I saw two birds at the window inside the Meeting House. The Meeting House had been locked and all the windows were shut. The birds were chimney swifts, and are found at the windows every once in a while. Their wings make them look like bats. And I thought: *How am I going to get them out?* Since the Meeting House has really tall ceilings, it's difficult to get the birds out. Also, if they've been in the chimney, they'll make a black mark if they brush up against the ceiling. So I walked over to the Sister's door to open it. When I turned around, the birds were gone! I hollered at Dixie, from the doorway: 'Dixie, get over here!' I walked down to the Administration Building; I was scared to death. I think it scared me because I saw something <u>physical</u>, and then it was gone; and I couldn't find it. I didn't have any explanation for it. *Where the heck did the birds go?* I didn't go by myself into the Meeting House for a while after that."

Besides the disappearing birds in the Meeting House, Beverly noticed that a window in the Meeting House displayed an unusual trait.

"When the administration office was in the upstairs of the Meeting House, I would go upstairs to go to the bathroom. The whole building was air conditioned then, and everything was closed. The window that was in the stairway on the Sister's side would <u>shake</u> every once in a while--not vibrate once or twice, but: 'Hmmmmmmm!' One night, I had to go on somewhere. I went upstairs to change from my Shaker clothes into my 'worldly' clothes. When I came down those stairs I thought the window was going to fly out of its frame. I looked at the window, and said, 'I'll put the clothes back on tomorrow, I'm going out.' As soon as I had said that it stopped, just <u>instantly</u>. And, I got to the point that when I came into the Meeting House on weekends, when I was alone, I would say as I went up the stairs, 'It's just me; don't worry about it, it's just me.' "

I asked Beverly, "What are your religious beliefs?"

Beverly: "I haven't had a history of seeing ghosts outside of Pleasant Hill. I don't go to church regularly, although I do consider myself to be a spiritual person. I was a total skeptic when I came here. But too many things have happened here that cannot be explained for me to still be a skeptic. I think the only time I've ever been frightened by a spirit here was when I was coming down the pike from the Trustee's Office. It was during an Elder Hostel, and it was at night and raining. I was walking to the West Family Dwelling. I knew somebody was walking behind me and I could <u>hear</u> them. When I turned around I couldn't see them, so I <u>ran</u>. I had heard footsteps and it made the hair stand up on the back of my neck. When I got down the pike by the Farm Deacon's Shop it was gone!"

Shaker worship was noted for its singing and dancing and channeling of spirits. Sometimes a Shaker worshiper would fall into a trance for days. The devout would thrash and shake out their sins. The group's charismatic expression would build up like a whirlwind.

"One lady came into the Meeting House; she was visibly shaken. She had stayed in the East Family Sister's Shop. She said, 'I have to talk to you, because I think I'm crazy. Last night at 10:48 (she had written down the time), I heard the most beautiful singing I have ever heard in my life. It was so soft and beautiful; the most beautiful female voice I ever heard. But you know what happened? It got louder

78

and louder and faster and faster. And finally I said, 'Why don't you shut up, you're going to wake up the whole building?' And it stopped! And I got up; I should have written down what I heard. But, the other strange thing is, I didn't understand what they were singing. It sounded like they were singing in a foreign language.' "

"I told her, 'A lot of times, with Shaker music, the songs will start out very softly and then they'll get faster and louder. They'll work themselves into a frenzy. It's called 'promiscuous' dancing, like if you'd go to a rock concert, and get all caught up in the music and feelings.' "

"And the woman said, 'Oh, thank God, I really thought I'd lost it. Since you've said that, I feel much better. Because I thought, whoever it was, I'd made them angry that I was here.' "

Randy Folger

Randy Folger

Originally from Washington state, Randy was the music director at Shakertown. He and his family moved to Kentucky when Randy was six years old, and he started working at Pleasant Hill in 1990. Randy soon became absorbed in research into Shaker history and theology, in addition to singing four concerts a day for the visitors. Randy was truly one of the most Shaker-like employees at Pleasant Hill. His character was gentle and the Shakers' music became very real when he sang their songs. Randy recorded two albums of Shaker music and transcribed a Pleasant Hill hymnal into modern notation. He was a busy worker, performing candlelight concerts, greeting and talking to the numerous guests who attend the Meeting House concerts, lecturing at Elder hostels and schools. In addition, Randy coordinated special events, workshops and music programming at the village.

Randy Folger passed on to spirit in 1999. I was in Seattle on vacation, not far from his birthplace, when I got the news that he had died in a car accident on the curvy highway near Shakertown. It was hard to accept our loss. So many people were touched by Randy's good nature and special gifts. And even though he smoked cigarettes, I still wanted to be around him, to just soak up his presence. Randy encouraged me to collect the Shaker ghost stories. He was very supportive, and a bit of a ghost hunter himself. In June, 1998, I went to Randy's home and recorded his ghost stories. The amazing thing about Randy, besides my never seeing him get angry, was his dedication to providing the visitors to the Meeting House with a unique sound and presence of someone who was very much...Shaker-like.

Randy performed the music concerts in the original Shakers' Meeting House. Its foundations are aligned with the Centre Family Dwelling, across the village street, and with the Trustee's Office, which is to the east. The floorboards of the Meeting House have seen and felt the dancing and whirling of the Shakers. The upper floor of the Meeting House had apartments for the ministry (a ruling body of two elders and two eldresses). Like the Centre Family Dwelling across the village pike, the Meeting House has two separate, exterior doors for separate entry by men and women. The Meeting House is the location of many unusual sights and sounds, heard and felt during both the day and night by employees and visitors to Shakertown.

"Often, I hear of some real weird experiences from the folks who come into the Meeting House for our music programs," Randy told me. "Sometimes, people will come up to me to ask questions after I sing and talk to everyone."

"One woman sent her family out of the Meeting House and waited until everybody was out of the room. She said, 'I just wanted to stick around and tell you something. When you were singing, I saw someone standing next to you. As you were singing, this 'person' got closer and closer to you until, finally, that person was <u>in</u> you and singing through you. I saw it just as plain as anything.' "

Randy, continuing, "Another time, I was doing one of the songs in the 'unknown tongue'. I was telling the group how the Shakers called that the 'angel's language' and that chances are, you wouldn't understand a <u>word</u> of that. But this one time that I sang in the unknown tongue, a woman in the front row had the most puzzled look on her face. After the program, she came up to me and said, 'You know, I've never been around the unknown tongue, I've never heard anything about it and I don't know anything about the Shakers. But when you said that was in the spirit language, I was floored, because I heard it in English.' "

"The woman told me the translation she had heard. It was definitely Shaker sentiments and Shaker theology. This song is over 150 years old and this woman had somehow received a translation! What was odd about this is that, as far as I know, the Shakers are the only denomination that practiced speaking in tongues who would write down the spirit language by phonetics."

Many visitors were entranced by Randy' singing. He delivered the Shaker music program with confidence and humble devotion, and in the question and answer time after his performance, he gracefully fielded a variety of queries about many aspects of Shaker life and worship.

"I've heard singing in the Meeting House, when there was nobody there. I have heard women's voices and men's voices. I've heard <u>beautiful</u> singing. I would hang out and read, in the little closet that had been off to one side, waiting for visitors to come into the Meeting House. As I sat in there, I would hear someone singing and walking around in the main room. But, I'd open the door and there would be nobody there. It was empty. So I knew spirits were there. The Meeting House seems to be the 'hot spot' of the village."

Randy added: "I've had other people say that they can hear somebody singing with me at times. They hear another voice, sometimes in harmony."

One time, Randy was in the Centre Family Dwelling, discussing spirit manifestations, when the banister on which he had his hand began to shake!

Does Pleasant Hill attract those who are seeking and open to spiritual wonder and metaphysical meanings? Randy tells of a woman who reported being 'guided' to come to Pleasant Hill.

"She was driving back from a woman's conference in Washington, DC, to her home in California. As she was headed south on Interstate 75, she saw a pillar of smoke or fire. She followed the pillar of 'smoke' to Shakertown. She said that the pillar disappeared when she turned onto Pleasant Hill property."

Are those really Shakertown employees, going about their jobs...?

Randy said that someone who works at the front desk told of one couple who had reported seeing a man dressed in Shaker garb, chopping wood in the early evening. The guests said, "Boy, you all go to great lengths to provide for an authentic atmosphere." They had seen the man from their room, looking out toward the back of the Ministry's workshop. But there had been no employee chopping wood!

Randy: "About three years ago a friend and I had been through some of the buildings at Shakertown, seeing if we could pick up on the spirits' presence. We were both interested in "ghost busting" and we were very curious as to what sort of spirits could be found. I've always been fascinated by stories of spirits and ghosts and we thought we'd try to find a few ourselves!

We really hadn't discovered much at all, so we started going to the Meeting House. We'd sit there, quietly, to see what might happen. I might sing some Shaker songs to encourage an appearance. Sometimes we would hear things. I remember one night, it wasn't raining and we heard: drip, drip, drip. But there's no water in the Meeting House at all. So we had no idea what was causing that, but we could hear it very plainly. Other times we would hear a footstep or two on the floorboards. But during those spirit searching sessions, we didn't hear anybody singing or dancing. We'd go and sit on the floor to try and connect with the 'vibrations'. We kept going, about once a week; it was kind of fun, though we weren't getting anywhere with our 'ghost busting'. Sometimes, we'd go up in the attic; there were no lights in there and it was very spooky. We felt, on the second floor, as if somebody was watching us."

Randy's tale becomes more focused: "Then, one night, we decided to go into the Meeting House. It was early fall and about midnight. The weather was calm. We went in and sat for a while. The first thing that we noticed was that one of the windows was totally black; you couldn't see out of it anymore. It was like a blind had been drawn over it. We could see out of the other windows; even though it was night, we could see the glow of a street lamp or whatever. But at this single window on the west wall that you could normally see out of, it was like there was something in front of it, like it was blocked out. I called it to my friend's attention and I said, 'What's that?' And he'd never seen anything like that before. It kind of gave us a weird feeling, like there was something in front of that window."

"The next thing we knew, we heard a wind begin to blow in the room. Outside was perfectly calm! It was calm when we went in, and we could look outside the windows and see that the leaves weren't moving. But we could hear this wind, starting up in the room. It started getting faster and faster, and louder and louder. It was circling, like a whirlwind.

We both said, 'What in the world is going on?' We were getting a little nervous by then, because it was picking up in intensity. It was getting louder and louder, and more violent all the time. I don't recall feeling it on my face; I was hearing it. So we actually got up and just left. We couldn't get out of there quick enough!"

"I locked the Meeting House door behind us and we came outside. We both walked away, passing in front of the Meeting House. I was thinking, *What in the world was going on in there? That was really a weird experience?!* And at that very moment, we heard a roar! To me, it sounded like a werewolf. I know that sounds crazy, but that's what I imagine a werewolf sounding like. It was very low sounding, just beastly. It was not, I guarantee you, a dog, or a coyote; and it wasn't a bobcat. It was right in front of the Centre Family Dwelling, on the other side of the fence, just low enough behind the fence so we couldn't see it. Within a second, we heard it again, but it was all the way down at the East Family Dwelling. It was unreal. That thing was there in front of the Centre Family Dwelling, and the next second it was down at the East Family Dwelling. I don't know how it did it, but this thing moved fast."

"The next day I came into work, and Larrie Curry (who is my boss and lives about two or three miles over the hills), said, 'Did you notice anything strange, last night? There was a disturbance in the natural world. I could feel it. My animals were going crazy, the dogs and the cats, were all going nuts. There was something going on.' "

"She asked me that out of the clear blue. Whatever we had tapped into, she was aware of it as well."

Speaking of blue, three weeks after Randy died, I had returned to my apartment in Lexington and I believe Randy paid me a visit. I was fast asleep in my bed when I was awakened by hearing my name being called. For some reason I got up and walked into my spare room, where there were wide, sliding glass door/windows. What amazed me, despite the obvious source of light from the moon late that night, was that the light was blue. There was no explanation for the blue light; nothing in the glass or in my room would bend the light from white to blue. I have a lot of experience from childhood as an amateur astronomer, with many hours logged at night observing moon, stars and planets. I had never before seen the light from the moon appearing in that color. I believe it was Randy visiting and saying farewell. Randy was my blue light special!

CHAPTER 4

Women in White

Shaker women in white attire have been sighted in a few places at Pleasant Hill. One story of a woman in white comes from Debbie Larkin. Debbie was the village herbalist. She is cheerful and bright, and very knowledgeable about the uses of herbs. She taught classes on the propagation, harvesting and storing of useful plants, and tended the Shaker herb garden which is on the west side of the Centre Family Dwelling near the central lane. On some of my visits to Shakertown, I would be drawn to the flowers and herbs. I wanted to learn more about herbs and to grown my own. The village, during the prime tourist season, could get a little busy. Those were good times for me to walk down to the lake, stroll out to Shawnee Run Creek, or if I had a shorter amount of time, step off the stone path and take in the beauty of the flowers and herbs. There were sunny chamomile flowers, mint, fragrant lavender, healing comphrey, and much more. I liked Debbie and she was generous with her time and knowledge. And as it turned out, she was in the special club of those who had a Shaker experience.

Debbie Larkin

"My encounter happened three or four summers ago. There had been a woman in the village the day before who was touring Shakertown. She lived fairly close to Pleasant Hill and she offered to donate some mullein and St. John's Wort plants to the village garden. I told her, 'Sure, we'd really appreciate it.' We have been given many plants from friends to put in the garden. She told me approximately when she would be coming that day; so I was looking and listening for her."

"I kept glancing down near the ticket booth from where I was working in the herb garden. It was late morning when I heard someone call my name. I looked toward the ticket booth, and I saw a woman dressed in white, waving at me. I realized that she was making a waving motion with her hand as though she wanted me to come. She was standing in the road near the ticket booth. I waved back at her, but it was too far to shout. So I indicated with my hands that I was coming down to meet with her."

"I put down my tools and started walking down there, but as I got closer I noticed that nobody was there! I had seen her very near the ticket booth so I went over to the ticket booth. I asked, 'Did you see a woman, dressed in white, with some plants for me?' I just assumed that this was the woman for whom I was waiting. But they said, 'No, nobody has been here for a while.' "

"I had seen her standing in the road between the ticket booth and the Farm Deacon's Shop so I went over to the Farm Deacon's Shop. Again I asked, 'Did a lady come in here with some plants for me?' "

"And they said, 'No, we haven't seen anyone.' "

"Then I went into the nearby Craft Store and I asked the shop workers, 'Have you seen a lady, dressed in white, with some plants for me?' "

"They answered, 'No, we haven't, it's very quiet here this morning.' "

"Nobody else had seen her!"

Debbie continues, "My friend, the woman with the plants, came later in the afternoon. She was dressed not in a white dress, but in blue jeans and a colored tee shirt. The first thing I said when she arrived was, 'Were you here earlier, and dressed in white, with some plants for me?' She said, 'No.'"

"This happened during the time when I put a lot of plants out into the garden, late May. That is the time when we often have a lot of students in the village, but there was not much traffic at all that morning."

"I told the staff curator, Larrie Curry, about the woman in white. I found out that there was a well-known skeptic of the paranormal who was visiting the village that day, and there was some speculation that the person's presence might prompt an appearance by the spirits."

"I felt blessed that they had picked me out to call upon. It had been very quiet around the village, and I was enjoying working in the garden that day. It was a strong impulse that had made me look up and turn to that direction. I wish that I had been paying more attention, but at the time I didn't know that I was having a "Shaker experience". I couldn't make out a face with the woman. I really should have thought it was odd that a woman who was bringing me plants would have been wearing a long white dress. I think that her head may have been covered. But now that I think back...it was almost like an aura, rather than being anything specific."

Other Shakertown employees have also seen mystery women.

Ruth Keller once worked as the front desk supervisor in the Ministry's Workshop building. Even though the upstairs room was locked, she would hear the sounds of someone walking there. She also tells of a night, about ten or eleven PM, when a security guard saw a lady at a window on the second floor of the Ministry's Workshop. Ruth stated that she was the only one in that building at that time, and she was downstairs.

Keith Hatter works at Pleasant Hill. He and another worker saw a ghost in the Trustee's Office. Keith reports that a female employee saw a woman with a full skirt going up the spiral staircase and she pointed out the figure to him.

At the West Family Dwelling, guests have reported seeing a woman who is standing at a third-floor window. They had noticed that she hadn't moved from the window for some time, so they inquired about her, thinking that she might need help.

Leslie Taylor is one of the many Centre Family Dwelling interpreters. She seems to be the 'no-nonsense type', and would not likely be fabricating a story of a spirit unless it was really there.

"One morning as I was coming to work at the Centre Family Dwelling, I walked around the side of the Meeting House as I do every morning. I came in from the parking lot around the east side of the

Meeting House. The front door of the Meeting House was open and I didn't think that was unusual. Normally somebody would be here ahead of me to open the door to the Meeting House. This was between 8:30 and 8:40 in the morning."

"As I walked around the building, I heard a female voice singing, and out of the corner of my eye I saw the edge of a white dress. At that time, the only person who would have been in there singing was Roberta Burnes. So I didn't think anything about it and walked on to the Centre Family Dwelling."

"I told everybody who came into the Centre Family Dwelling that day, 'Don't miss the singing performances in the Meeting House, because Roberta Burnes is here and she is absolutely wonderful!' "

"Well, about three o'clock that afternoon, I left the Centre Family Dwelling to go across the village street. Randy Folger, the music director, came out of the front of the Meeting House. He said, 'Now, do I look like Roberta Burnes?' "

"He informed me that Roberta had not been on the property that day! I had heard a beautiful singing voice, but it had not been Roberta."

Sarah Moran, a dining room waitress, reports that, "Last year a supervisor told me that she had seen a white figure that was kind of floating down the stairs in the Trustee's Office building. She saw it for only a few seconds."

Roberta Burnes might be said to be one of <u>the</u> women in white, as she wears a white dress when she performs as a singer. Roberta sings with a powerful and clear voice. She fills the Meeting House with the idealistic feeling of Shaker sentiment through their songs and her singing. Roberta has worked part-time as a music interpreter for many years. She sings and performs Shaker music programs with the Kentucky Humanities Program, and has recorded a compact disc of Shaker women's music. I had been a house sitter in the summer of 1997 for Roberta and her husband John, when they went to the British Isles. Roberta struck me as a sort of Renaissance person, good with science and also good with the arts.

Roberta shared with me that a few times she had been baffled by some invisible accompaniment to her singing.

"A couple of years ago, I happened to be singing 'Amazing Grace' for a daytime public performance. As I sang, I noticed musical tones contributed by the audience. It was like a choir of angels who were singing 'ooo'. I thought, *this audience is good.*"

"After my performance, the folks from the audience came up to greet me and thank me for my singing. They said, 'You were really great with that song.' And I said to them, 'So were you.'

But they said, 'We weren't singing. There was nobody else singing but you!' "

"Another time, after that, when I sang 'Amazing Grace' I focused on the spirit accompaniment that I again started to hear, but it went away."

"Sometime later I was doing a candlelight performance. I was singing the Shaker song, 'The Savior's Universal Prayer'. This time it was my husband John who heard the choir-like sound, and I didn't hear it at all. When we compared notes, we agreed that it sounded a lot like a choir of women's voices that you hear in those 'hokey' old black and white movies, when the voices come in at the end of the film. There had been many layers on top of my voice."

Tall cedar tree

CHAPTER 5

The Mystery of Holy Sinai's Plain

The casual visitor to Shakertown at Pleasant Hill can be easily impressed by the visible achievements of the Shakers. One can see wonderful buildings that are 175-years old, stone fences, a road leading from the Kentucky River, and hundreds of artifacts of an industrious life. Visitors can view the incredible craftsmanship of the spiral staircase in the Trustee's Office and marvel at the organization of the production of various Shaker industries such as, silk, seeds, boxes and brooms. The Shaker's vibrant spiritual life, however, is a greater challenge to deduce. From journal accounts and visitors' recollections, we know a little of how they danced and sang. They were greatly inspired and tried to live the highest of moral ideals.

On Shaker property near the main village laid a mysterious site sacred to the Shakers. This secret

Shaker worship site was called Holy Sinai's Plain. This sacred place has long been abandoned and the evidence of its existence destroyed by the Shakers. But archaeologists and researchers found the Holy Plain in the spring of 1997.

There are a few stories of spirit activity connected with Holy Sinai's Plain and even its discovery. This was the singular location where the 'worldly people' could not participate in witnessing the Shaker's worship. The Shakers experienced a charismatic revival from 1837 until 1847. Starting in the community of Watervliet in New York State, incredible visions and spirit personalities were seen. Many of those who became channels for the spirits were young girls (often between the ages of 12 and 15). They were called 'inspired ones' or 'instruments', and would often speak in the 'unknown tongue'. This was the angels' language, some of which was recorded in Shaker journals and put into song. Sarah Pool was the first person of that revival to become an instrument at Pleasant Hill. The messages were consistent with the basic Shaker theology of obedience, humility, repentance, subjugation of the flesh, and orderly life. From their trance state, the inspired ones related messages from Mother Ann and people of the Bible. There were messages from historic men and women: George Washington, Benjamin Franklin, William Penn, Tecumseh, and even God Himself. Invisible gifts would be "distributed" to aid in the worship and in the devotion of the Shaker life: drums, trumpets, fifes, etc.

The Mount Lebanon (New York) community sent out a directive to each Shaker village to set apart a secret worship place some distance from the meeting house. The ministry at Pleasant Hill dedicated a plot of land to be their Holy Sinai's Plain. (The Shaker villages had different names chosen for their sacred worship sites). It was noted in the journals as being one-half mile southeast of the Meeting House. Common to these special sites in the various Shaker societies was a leveled spot away from their village, a neat presentation of the sacred circle. (Pleasant Hill's was sown in bluegrass and had neat, wood fencing), a pool of water and a sacred stone and/or altar.

Holy Sinai's Plain was not visited often. It was for special observances and not open to outside visitors. It is in fact noted that some of the altar stones had a curse carved into the stone noting detrimental consequences for those who might disturb the sacred location. After a period of about ten years, the charismatic guidance that had inspired the revival and the making of the holy ground, indicated that this special time was ending. The villages were instructed to destroy the altar stones, tear down the fence and to hide all evidence of their location and use.

After his "whirlwind" experience in the Meeting House, Randy Folger decided to leave off "ghost busting" in the Meeting House. One day he hiked around to investigate the area where Holy Sinai's Plain was reported to be. From Shaker journal entries, some possible locations were looked at on Shaker land that lay on the other side of US Highway 68. Randy and a friend had some baffling experiences in that area of land.

"We started going down and looking for Holy Sinai's Plain at night; we always had to look for these things at night. We'd go down and park on the river road because the gate would be locked at night. We'd climb over the gate and walk down to the place I used to think was the Plain. We'd go down the road a little way. Right before we'd get into the woods, there was another gate. Then we would climb over the gate and walk up a little hill and there was a beautiful plain."

"One time, when I was walking the old Shaker river road, I felt somebody watching me as I was coming back from the river. This was during the day. I looked back up to the top of the cliffs, and there was somebody dressed in Shaker costume up there, looking down at me. I said, 'Hello!' and the person backed away from the edge of the cliff. I walked all the way to the top and I could see this person, whoever it was, over in the line of trees. As I walked the figure would walk parallel to me. He never would approach me or say hello. I tried to speak to him again. I tried to approach him one time, and he would walk off, into the woods. I have no idea what that was all about."

In addition to seeing the silent Shaker, Randy heard once again from the invisible beast that he and his friend had heard in the village.

"On our second night, hanging out at that spot I thought to be Holy Sinai's Plain, all of a sudden we heard a wolf-like growl. It was the same beast that we had heard in the village after the whirlwind in the Meeting House about a week before. It sounded just as loud and just as angry as when we heard it in the village. We had flashlights with us and we shone our flashlights in the direction from which the sound came, but it was nowhere. There was nothing there; it was empty space. The sound had been right there, but when we shone the lights it was gone! Then we heard it again maybe a mile farther off."

"My neighbor, who lives two doors down, is a biology teacher at the local high school. He enjoys studying animals. About a week after hearing that wolf-like sound he came to visit me. He said, 'Man, I've been hearing the weirdest sounds at night. My wife and I will be sitting out on the patio and we hear an animal we've <u>never</u> heard before! I can't imagine what it is.' So I don't know what this thing was, but it apparently was down at his house a night or two. If it was indeed an animal, how did it relocate itself to sound out again so quickly? And why would it be close to us to begin with? Usually animals take off when they hear you coming. My friend actually took someone else to the same spot and they heard this thing too."

At Pleasant Hill, in our modern era, no physical evidence was found for many years to pinpoint the sacred Plain. But in 1997 the archaeologists got closer and closer to its discovery. When a worker with a compass crossed over one spot of land, he noticed the compass spinning wildly, then freezing still. The compass, despite some knocks to encourage its regular performance, would not work any more. With bulldozer and back hoe and persistence, the workers uncovered the "shadow" of the potholes of the Shaker's oval fence that must have surrounded their Holy Sinai's Plain. The posts had evidently been removed; but the soil replaced into those holes was a bit darker. This gave the archaeologists evidence needed to confirm the discovery of the secret worship site. One of the bulldozers would not start up for some time, and in the village itself some unusual occurrences were noted that day.

That summer I gathered around the trench with other Shaker singers for a photograph for the Lexington newspaper, the Herald-Leader. We sang and we tried to project ourselves into the respectful role of latter day interpreters. But overtime, I heard some intriguing stories of how perhaps the excavation of the site might have upset the Shaker spirits. And later, the singers debated the pros and cons of performing at Holy Sinai's Plain. We had a number of programs where we marched from the village, from outside the Meeting House, to Holy Sinai's Plain, singing all the way. Then we danced and sang at that sacred Shaker site.

Beverly Rogers and two other Shakertown employees had some strange experiences the day of the discovery of Holy Sinai's plain.

"I was doing a Meeting House tour that day," Beverly said. "I had unlocked and opened the back door and I was standing in the hallway. I heard voices and walking upstairs. I wondered if Susan Hughes had brought in some people to show them the attic. I went up to the second floor, but I didn't find anybody. I came back downstairs, getting ready to go into main first floor room, and I heard the same thing again. I thought, *maybe they were on the third floor.* So I went back up through the second floor to the attic and I found no one there. When I saw Larrie Curry three or four days later I told her about this encounter."

Larrie said, 'Do you realize that was the day they found the first three postholes in Sinai's Plain?' "

The white circling fence of Holy Sinai's Plain

105

Carol Zahn, an interpreter at the Centre Family Dwelling, reports that Larrie Curry and Randy Folger offered a tour of Holy Sinai's Plain to some of the employees. They packed up in cars and drove to the nearby site. Just as they got out of their cars at the sacred site, an unusual sleet storm fell upon them. When they got back to their cars to leave Holy Sinai's Plain, the storm suddenly stopped. Carol questions the strange and isolated storm that fell that day. She wonders if they had ignored the employee gossip about a possible stone altar curse forbidding anyone to revisit that sacred Shaker site. Perhaps the Shaker spirits were restless and had not approved of the excavation?

Two Pleasant Hill employees had an astonishing experience when Holy Sinai's Plain was discovered. Rose Sorrell worked at Shakertown for 23 years. After two years there, she continued to work in the craft store at its new location in the Carpenter's Shop. Rose and another employee were in the basement storage room below the craft store. The storage room is reached by descending spiral stairs from the sales floor. The room is narrow with an exit door to the ground level at its end. There is a kitchen table and microwave for employee breaks. And there are long shelves for storing shop merchandise. Rose was standing by the kitchen table, talking to an employee who was about to go out the exit door.

Reproduction Shaker table

They were discussing some of the spirit world's possibilities, when a small round walnut candle stand lifted and moved through the air. It had been safely stored upside down on the desk. Rose reports that it spun about eight feet across the room and split and broke when it landed. Her coworker was nowhere near the table. A few minutes later, a wooden hanger went flying off from its secure place, bouncing and spinning to the floor.

Rose asked her coworker, "Did you do that?" He replied, "I don't think so!"

"One woman, who is a Centre Family Dwelling interpreter, grew up in the area of Pleasant Hill. She remembers the area of Holy Sinai's Plain feeling different to her and her family.

"When we would walk up to the gate to that area, I wouldn't want to go through the gate and further along there. I got a 'fluttery' feeling."

The maintenance worker called 'Tucker' reports that "mechanical things go nuts in the two to three weeks before a tour of Holy Sinai's Plain."

Tucker rotates with the other workers on the night maintenance duty. "Up until two months ago, when the heat got so bad and they canceled the trips to Holy Sinai's Plain, we would be running all night to fix things. The air handlers (heating/cooling systems) would burn out before they were very old. Fire alarms sounded without any fires. Someone would say that there was probably dust or spiders that got into the fire alarm to make it go off. But we'd use an air hose to blow out whatever might be in there, and the air hose wouldn't dislodge anything. There are outside lights on tall poles that we have to get up to with a ladder. We would find those lights up there had been unscrewed. Since the summer heat stopped the tours, we now only get about one or two calls per night."

Tucker adds "just about every worker in the village has turned lights off and later discovered that they would be back on again."

Pleasant Hill Singers   Photo by Joel Schulman
at Holy Sinai's Plain

East staircase of twin spiral staircases,
viewed from third floor

CHAPTER 6

The Shaker Experience

When I strive to explain the happenings at Pleasant Hill, I can't separate the spirit phenomena there from the plethora of ghost tales that are experienced in the greater world. The belief structure of the Shakers must be taken into consideration, but in the end, one must tackle the universal questions of life, death, and spiritual realities. For me, the Shaker ghost stories also occurred in the personal framework, my intimate experience with the Shaker singers, and with the deaths of some family and friends during the years from 1996 to 2002. We lost several Shaker singers and they were believers in the spirit occurrences. In attempting to understand the framework of the ghostly experiences that people had, I not only interviewed those that were willing, but also I heard the opinions of the skeptics. Some of those skeptics had worked years at Shakertown and admitted to having seen no ghosts at all. I invited three psychics to Shakertown and we walked through the village and about the land. Ultimately, like most of life, our experience at Pleasant Hill may be somewhat projective—we find what we believe, we experience what we already know.

I feel encouraged by hearing from others that they have had their Shaker experiences. In my world view, I believe that people's essence is saved not destroyed at death. The spirit is active and often desires to communicate values, thoughts, feelings and love itself beyond the grave.

The devotional power of love transforms lives. And according to the Bible, brought the dead back to life. If our thoughts determine our reality, then look at the sayings and beliefs of the United Society of Believers in Christ's Second Appearing.

The Shakers believed that heaven had united with earth; they were living and breathing the reality of Christ returned and of the Millennium.

" Love fills my heart and hope my breast
With joy I yield my breath.

'Tis love that drives my chariot wheels,
And death must yield to love."

Shaker Jemima Blanchard, 1845

The Shakers believed that they did not need a priestly class; the Spirit of God and His inspiring agencies spoke directly to them.

"That divinely vitalized beings possess a corresponding power I have not the smallest doubt; indeed, I have the most undoubted assurance that all such, whether in or out of the body, possess that power."

Shaker Daniel Frazer, 1880

The Shakers allowed and respected spiritual mediums among their ranks. The Shakers were entranced, "slain in the spirit", channeled prophecy and words of wisdom, were given spirit instruments and received songs and music from a spiritual source. It is certainly possible that the Shaker work world was a direct spiritual gift, including the inspiration for their inventions. They saw visions and angels. Mother Ann performed miraculous healings.

"When we know that mediumistic spiritualism is only the development of a natural faculty, the same as singing or speaking, we assign it to its legitimate place."

Shaker Elder Benjamin Dunlavy, 1884

The Shakers applied a clarity and discipline of mind and body to their assumption that the Spirit of Wisdom was the core organizing factor of their lives. Without a clutter of personal possessions and having relinquished sexual attachments, the Shakers were free to live their cherished mental ideals of love and service.

> "The spirit world is a world of causes;
> thus, of effects. *Mind* is the primal
> cause of all material existence.
> Our physical being is in every way
> subservient to the spirit that animates it..."

> Anonymous Shaker

The Shakers thus saw little differentiation between the world of matter and the domain of heavenly spirit. All of the life they were co-creating with divine spirit was united in the overriding presence of God's freely given love.

> "The material worlds! The spiritual
> worlds! Why, is it all not all spirit, in
> different stages of unfoldment...?"

> *The Shaker*, 1841

With the spirit world ever present and at times hardly discernible from mortal involvement, the Shakers had clearly constructed a Zion (heaven on earth). Why leave Zion, or why not return after the passage we refer to as death? As they opened channels of energy to the greater spiritual world, perhaps they were creating the means for their own spirits to return, by those same energy circuits. The Shakers would then return to be the guardians of a sacred place and spiritual retreat.

"Let thirsty, hungry, starving Zion
so live and labor, and they will have the
key to unlock the heavens, and draw
from her sacred fountains blessings to the
satisfaction of every heaven-born soul."

The Shaker Manifesto, 1881

Could it be that the spirits at Shakertown are real and act in our current time and dimension and have an independent though cooperative volition? In other words, we seek them and they seek us and we meet as we are able. Many of the Shaker ghost stories from Pleasant Hill point out common experiential attitude adjustments. For instance, there was an employee who was a skeptic and became a believer in ghosts through numerous experiences. Those who might have needed a boost of spiritual faith heard beautiful and inspirational singing. One woman insists she saw an angel, who exhorted the virtues of the Shaker Way. Randy Folger tried 'ghost busting' and <u>he</u> was busted (The Whirlwind story)! Why would a Shaker spirit grab a hold of a guest in their bed? Maybe they and only they knew what the message might have been, like interpreting a dream for our life only. The guardian of the graveyard could have been trying to steer the three young men straight with a little well timed boost of fear. Or perhaps the Shaker spirits are simply proof that we continue to live past death; and we pick up over there precisely where we leave from here.

Wall Lamp

MEMORIAM

Pleasant Hill Employees

I am grateful for the assistance and friendship of many in the creating of this book; some of those who helped were singers and/or interpreters at Shakertown. Some of these kind souls passed away while this book was being written:

Mrs. Mary Lee Woford, Interpreter
for 24 years, April 1998

Randy Folger, Music Director,
9 years, July 1999

Carol Zahn, Interpreter and
Pleasant Hill Singer, 2002

Edna Quinn, Interpreter
8 Years, 2002

Lower road toward Mill Ruins

In Gratitude

Friends who encouraged me to write this book of Shaker Ghost Stories may not have realized how their support was valued. These friends include: Susan and Chuck Creacy, Randy Folger, Mary Brinkman, Normandi Ellis, Sarah Thomas, all of the Pleasant Hill Singers, Rose Sorrell, Don Pelly, the administration and employees of Shakertown, and the visitors to Pleasant Hill—those who shared their ghost stories. I am grateful to the Pleasant Hill Trustees and all who worked in small and large ways to restore Shakertown and provide a haven for learning, meditation and insight.

I also thank the Shakers. Their hard work and vision provided a sturdy nineteenth century village of exceptional construction. Their many manuscripts of original songs continue to provide joy and inspiration for those open to breathing their words. And their example of simple lives of service gives us hope when we are bounced around by a busy world.

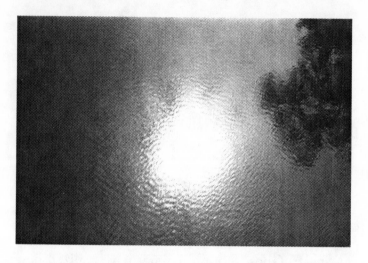

Sun reflection in Shaker pond

About the Author

Thomas Freese's varied experiences—with writing, arts, storytelling, teaching, and healing—contribute to the creative wisdom that shows in his work. He studied Spanish in Mexico, managed a Mexican import store in Santa Fe, was a movie extra, played harmonica and guitar, created his own jewelry business, taught around Kentucky as an artist-in-residence, illustrated books, sang with the Pleasant Hill Singers, performed as a storyteller at schools and libraries, and earned a Masters Degree in Expressive Therapies.

Thomas has written since 1998 for the Chevy Chaser and Southsider Magazines, in Lexington, KY, (www.chevychaser.com). He writes both feature articles and the monthly column "Day Trips". For the Day Trips, Thomas travels throughout Kentucky and surrounding states to report on fun and intriguing places and people. When traveling and making new friends, Thomas is always keen to hear about the experiences of others; this desire to promote the stories and lives of those he meets led him to collect the ghost stories from Shakertown at Pleasant Hill.

Thomas Freese believes that material, mortal life, shows but a small portion of the greater reality of our nature, existence and potential. By collecting and writing Shaker Ghost Stories, he endeavors to encourage kindred spirits to acknowledge their own stories, particularly those out of the ordinary moments that are special and help us to see with eyes of inner truth. As an Art Therapist and Counselor, Thomas Freese practices and promotes the safe, nurturing and effective expression of inner creativity, truth, and soul journey. He has collected many more ghost stories in addition to the Shaker Ghost Stories; those tales will surely appear in future books!

Printed in the United States
119275LV00001B/19-114/A

9 781420 850727